CHARACTER OPTIONS

CREDITS

Writer/Designer Monte Cook
Additional Writing Shanna Germain, Rob Schwalb
Lead Editor Shanna Germain
Editor and Proofreader Ray Vallese
Cover Artist Kieran Yanner
Graphic Designer Sarah Robinson

Artists Jason Engle, Brandon Leach, Eric Lofgren, Patrick McEvoy, Brynn Metheney, Michael Perry, Michael Phillippi, Hugo Solis, Shane Tyree, Ben Wootten, Kieran Yanner

Cartographer Christopher West

Monte Cook Games Editorial Board Scott C. Bourgeois, David Wilson Brown, Eric Coates, Ryan Klemm, Jeremy Land, Laura Wilkinson, George Ziets

TABLE OF CONTENTS

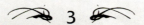

INTRODUCTION

Needs No Weapon,
page 68
Masters Insects,
page 65
Constantly Evolves,
page 55

What are character options? Simply put, they're more choices for players when creating their characters. Why would a game focused mainly on story care about more mechanical stuff for characters, though? The Numenera corebook stresses that this isn't a game about min-maxing your character, creating the "perfect" character builds, and so on. In fact, one of the things I love most about the game is how little time character creation takes. You can sit down at the table without a character and literally be playing the game ten minutes later.

So why does this book exist? Simple. Another thing that Numenera stresses is the ability for players to play the characters they want to play. That's why the skill system is so open ended, for example, and why so much leeway and fluidity is built into the various abilities and whatnot that a character might have. More choices give more room for character customization.

Location-Based
Descriptors, page 31

Foci, page 51

More choices also help to show the breadth of the setting. Take a look at the Foci chapter of this book. Sure, some of the foci, like Needs No Weapon, simply make sense and are worthy additions to the game. But Masters Insects and Constantly Evolves really speak to the weird and unusual elements of the Ninth World setting.

This aspect of character creation is so important to us that we created a new kind of descriptor, one that relates to where you're from and how that affects who you are. Whether your characters grew up among the automatons in the Weal of Baz or are deeply committed to Malevich's codes of justice and mercy, their homeland becomes an important part of their motivations and skills. You can find more examples of these location-based descriptors in the Location-Based Descriptors section.

So there are new foci and new descriptors, but you won't find new types here. I don't think we've come anywhere close to fully exploring the glaive, the nano, and the jack. (I won't say "never," but we have no plans to create new types in the foreseeable future.) That said, I think there are acres of room for additional options in the tier-based abilities

I AM AN *ADJECTIVE NOUN* WHO *VERBS*

As a reminder, creating your Numenera character is as easy as building a simple sentence. In fact, it *is* building a simple sentence: "I am a [fill in an adjective here] [fill in a noun here] who [fill in a verb here.]" Thus: "I am an *adjective noun* who *verbs*."

For example, you might say, "I am a Mad glaive who Constantly Evolves" or "I am a Vengeful nano who Consorts With the Dead."

In this sentence, the adjective is your *descriptor*.

The noun is your character *type*.

The verb is your *focus*.

For complete details on creating a Numenera character, including stats, tiers, skills, character sheets, and a character creation walkthrough, see the Numenera corebook (especially Part 2: Characters).

that each type chooses. So in the Character Type Options chapter, you'll find a lot of new fighting moves, esoteries, and tricks of the trade to further customize your chosen type.

The book finishes off with a few guidelines for GMs to allow for even more character customization, if the players wish it.

I hope you find this book to be a useful and fun addition to your games, and that it helps you create a character that gives you hours of joy at the table.

COREBOOK CALLOUTS

Throughout this book, you'll see page references to various items accompanied by this symbol. These are page references to the Numenera corebook, where you can find additional details about that item, place, creature, or concept. It isn't necessary to look up the referenced items in the corebook, but doing so will provide useful information for character creation and gameplay.

Character Type Options, page 6

Fighting moves, page 29

Esoteries, page 35

Tricks of the trade, page 42

CHARACTER TYPE OPTIONS

Defense roll, page 16
Edge, page 20
Effort, page 21

The three character types in Numenera—glaive, nano, and jack—are the very heart of the character creation system. Character types grant PCs special abilities at each new tier. Using these abilities often costs points from your stat Pools; the cost is listed in parentheses after the ability name. Your Edge in the appropriate stat can reduce the cost of the ability, but remember that you can apply Edge only once per action.

Sometimes the point cost for an ability has a + sign after the number. For example, the cost might be given as "2+ Intellect points." That means you can spend more points or more levels of Effort to improve the ability further.

Many special abilities grant a character the option to perform an action that she couldn't normally do, such as projecting rays of cold or attacking multiple foes at once. Using one of these abilities is an action unto itself, and the end of the ability's description says "Action" to remind you. It also might provide more information about when or how you perform the action.

Some special abilities allow you to perform a familiar action—one that you can already do—in

a different way. For example, an ability might let you wear heavy armor, reduce the difficulty of Speed defense rolls, or add 2 points of fire damage to your weapon damage. These abilities are called enablers. Using one of these abilities is not considered an action. Enablers either function constantly (such as being able to wear heavy armor, which isn't an action) or happen as part of another action (such as adding fire damage to your weapon damage, which happens as part of your attack action). If a special ability is an enabler, the end of the ability's description says "Enabler" to remind you.

GLAIVE: NEW FIGHTING MOVES

Glaives can add these new fighting moves into the mix when selecting their fighting moves for each tier.

FIRST-TIER GLAIVE

Danger Sense (1 Speed point): The difficulty of your initiative roll is reduced by one step. Enabler.

Fleet of Foot: If you succeed at a difficulty 2 Speed-based running task, you can move a short distance *and* take an action in the same round. Enabler.

Goad (2 Might points): After you successfully attack a creature, the difficulty of Speed defense rolls made by all others against attacks by that creature is decreased by one step until the end of the next round. Enabler.

Muscles of Iron (2 Might points): For the next ten minutes, all Might-based actions other than attack rolls that you attempt have their difficulty reduced by one step. Enabler.

Opportunist: You have an asset on any attack roll you make against a creature that has been attacked at some point during the round and is within immediate range. Enabler.

Overwatch (1 Intellect point): You use a ranged weapon to target a limited area (such as a doorway, a hallway, or the eastern side of the clearing) and make an attack against the next viable target to enter that area. This works like a wait action, but you also negate any benefit the target would have from cover, position, surprise, range, illumination, or visibility. Further, you inflict 1 additional point of damage with the attack. You can remain on overwatch as long as you wish, within reason. Action.

Quick Draw (2 Speed points): You use an action to make an attack with a thrown light weapon. You then draw another light weapon and make another thrown attack against the same target or a different one. Action.

Surging Confidence (1 Might point): When you use an action to make your first recovery roll of the day, you immediately gain another action. Enabler.

SECOND-TIER GLAIVE

Avalanche (2 Might points): When you get a minor effect or a major effect for an attack using a weapon you wield in two hands, you deal the extra damage and you knock the creature down. Enabler.

Block (3 Speed points): You automatically block the next melee attack made against you within the next minute. Action to initiate.

Bloodlust (3 Might points): If you take down a foe, you can move a short distance, but only if you move toward another foe. You don't need to spend the points until you know that the foe is down. Enabler.

Find an Opening (1 Intellect point): You use trickery to find an opening in your foe's defenses. Make a Speed roll against one creature within immediate range. On a success, the difficulty of your next attack against that creature before the end of the next round is reduced by one step. Action.

Guarded Attack: While you're using a shield when you make an attack with a melee weapon, you can choose to increase the difficulty of the roll by one step. You then decrease the difficulty of all Speed defense rolls you make by one step until the end of the round. Enabler.

Mighty Blow (2 Might points): You strike two foes with a single blow. Make separate attack rolls for each foe, but both attacks

Might, page 20
Asset, page 16
Wait, page 102
Surprise, page 95
Minor effect, page 88
Major effect, page 88

count as a single action in a single round. You remain limited by the amount of Effort you can apply on one action. Anything that modifies your attack or damage applies to both of these attacks. Action.

Recovery roll, page 94

Quick Recovery: Your second recovery roll (usually requiring ten minutes) takes only a single action, just like the first roll. Enabler.

Sense Ambush: You are never treated as surprised by an attack. Enabler.

Shield Bash (3 Might points): If you make a melee attack and you're using a shield, you can also make an attack with your shield as a part of the same action. Any Effort or modifications that apply to your main attack apply to the shield attack as well. A shield counts as a medium weapon. Action.

Stand Watch (2 Intellect points): While standing watch (mostly remaining in place for

an extended period of time), you unfailingly remain awake and alert for up to eight hours. During this time, you are trained in perception tasks as well as stealth tasks to conceal yourself from those who might approach. Action to initiate.

THIRD-TIER GLAIVE

Brutality (3 Might points): When using a heavy weapon, you make a slight adjustment to clip your foe as you draw your weapon back for another swing. Thus, if you miss with your attack, your target still takes 1 point of damage from the clip. Enabler.

Daring Escape (5 Speed points): You dodge an attack and trick your attacker into hitting someone else by accident. If you succeed on a Speed defense roll, you can force the attacker to instead attack a different creature within immediate range. Enabler.

Deadly Aim (3 Speed points): For the next minute, all ranged attacks you make inflict 2 additional points of damage. Action to initiate.

Fury (3 Might points): For the next minute, all melee attacks you make inflict 2 additional points of damage. Action to initiate.

Inner Defense: You are trained in any task to resist the ability of another to discern your true feelings, beliefs, or plans. You are likewise trained in resisting torture, telepathic intrusion, and mind control. Enabler.

Run and Fight (4 Might points): You can move a short distance and make a melee attack. The attack inflicts 2 additional points of damage. Action.

Seize Opportunity (4 Speed points): If you succeed on a Speed defense roll to resist an attack, you gain an action. You can use it immediately even if you have already taken a turn in the round. If you use this action to attack, the difficulty of your attack is reduced by one step. You don't take an action during the next round. Enabler.

Stone Breaker: Your attacks against objects inflict 4 additional points of damage when you use a melee weapon that you wield in two hands. Enabler.

FOURTH-TIER GLAIVE

Ambusher: When you attack a creature that has not yet acted during the first round of combat, the difficulty of your attack is reduced by one step. Enabler.

Confounding Banter (4 Intellect points): You spew a stream of nonsense to distract a foe. Make an Intellect roll against a creature within

immediate range. On a success, the difficulty of the defense roll against the creature's next attack before the end of the next round is reduced by one step. Action.

Debilitating Strike (4 Speed points): You make an attack to deliver a painful or debilitating strike. The difficulty of that attack is increased by one step. If it hits, the creature takes 2 additional points of damage at the end of the next round, and the difficulty of defense rolls to resist its attacks is decreased by one step until the end of the next round. Action.

Hardy: You are immune to disease, and the difficulty of Might defense rolls against poison effects is reduced by two steps. Enabler.

Momentum: If you use an action to move, your next attack made using a melee weapon before the end of the next round inflicts 2 additional points of damage. Enabler.

Precise Strike: When you attack using a weapon, the difficulty of your attack is decreased by one step, and the damage is reduced by 3 points (minimum 0 points). Enabler.

Precise Timing: If you take the same action for three rounds in a row, on the third round (and every consecutive round thereafter), the difficulty is reduced by one step. Actions might include bashing a door, swimming across a raging river, or attacking the same foe. Enabler.

FIFTH-TIER GLAIVE

Hard Target: If you move a short distance or farther on your turn, the difficulty of all Speed defense rolls is reduced by one additional step. Enabler.

Inverse Attrition: In every round of combat after the first, you gain a +1 bonus to damage. This bonus increases every other round. So on the second and third rounds, you inflict 1 additional point of damage. On the fourth and fifth rounds, you inflict 2 additional points of damage. You must be a participant in the combat, and you must be fully aware and take an action in a round for it to count toward an increase in damage. Enabler.

Killing Blow (5 Might points): You exploit your enemy's diminished vitality to deliver a killing blow. Make a melee attack and inflict 6 additional points of damage if your target is at one-half health or less. Action.

Press (6 Might points): You drive a foe back from your companions. Make an attack with a melee weapon. In addition to inflicting damage, both you and the target move a

short distance together so you remain within immediate range of each other. Action.

Riposte (6 Speed points): When you succeed on a Speed defense roll against an attack from a creature within immediate range, you can immediately make an attack on that creature, or you can gain an asset for the next attack you make on it before the end of the next round. Enabler.

SIXTH-TIER GLAIVE

Combat Trance (7 Might points): You empty your mind of all distractions to let your instincts take over. For one minute, you can take two actions each round, but only one of those actions can be an attack. Action to initiate.

Run Through Walls (6 Might points): When you use an action to move and you move up to an obstacle, you can make a Might roll. The GM sets the difficulty based on the material from which the object is made. If you succeed, you smash through the obstacle and leave behind a hole large enough for others to move through. Enabler.

Spring Away (5 Speed points): Whenever you succeed on a Speed defense roll, you can immediately move up to a short distance. You cannot use this ability more than once in a given round. Enabler.

Many glaives believe that the best way to win a fight is to maintain a strong defense—in other words, to be the last combatant standing. Others believe that simply being strong enough or skilled enough to put down their opponent quickly is the best way. The truth is, it depends on the strengths and weaknesses of one's opponent, and in the Ninth World, those things can vary wildly.

Esotery, page 35

NANO: NEW ESOTERIES

Nanos can add these new esoteries into the mix when selecting their esoteries for each tier.

FIRST-TIER NANO

Aggression (2 Intellect points): You reach into the mind of a character and unlock his more primitive instincts. Choose one character within short range. That character has an asset on Might-based attack rolls. The effect lasts for one minute. Action to initiate.

Distortion (2 Intellect points): You modify how a willing creature reflects light for one minute. Choose a creature within short range. The target rapidly shifts between its normal appearance and a blot of darkness. The target has an asset on Speed defense rolls until the effect wears off. Action to initiate.

Erase Memories (3 Intellect points): You reach into a creature's mind to make it forget. Choose one creature within immediate range and make an Intellect roll. On a success, you erase up to the last five minutes of the creature's memory. The creature forgets what it experienced during that time. Action.

Far Step (2 Intellect points): You leap through the air and land some distance away. You can jump up, down, or across to anywhere you choose within long range if you have a clear and unobstructed path to that location. You land safely. Action.

Machine Interface (2 Intellect points): The difficulty of discerning the level, function, and activation of powered numenera devices that you touch is decreased by one step for one minute. Enabler.

Mental Link (1+ Intellect point): You open a pathway to another creature's mind via a light touch, which allows you to transmit thoughts and images to each other. In other words, you can communicate with each other without having to speak. The mental link remains regardless of distance and lasts for one hour. Instead of applying Effort to decrease the difficulty of this esotery, you can apply Effort to extend the duration by one hour for each level of Effort. Action to initiate.

Resonance Field (1 Intellect point): Faint lines in a color you choose form a tracery over your entire body and emit faint light. The effect lasts for one minute. Whenever a creature within immediate range makes an attack against you, the pattern energizes to block the attack. You can make an Intellect defense roll in place of the defense roll you would normally make. If you do so and you get a minor effect, the creature attacking you takes 1 point of damage. If you get a major effect, the creature attacking you takes 4 points of damage. Action to initiate.

Sculpt Flesh (2 Intellect points): You cause a willing creature's fingers to lengthen into claws and her teeth to grow into fangs by sculpting her flesh. The effect lasts for ten minutes. The damage dealt by the target's unarmed strikes increases to 4 points. Action.

SECOND-TIER NANO

Cutting Light (2 Intellect points): You emit a thin beam of energized light from your hand in immediate range. This inflicts 5 points of damage to a single foe. It is even more effective when used against immobile, nonliving targets. It slices up to 1 foot (0.3 m) of any material that is level 6 or less. The material can be up to 1 foot thick. Action.

Fetch (3 Intellect points): You cause an object to disappear and reappear in your hands or somewhere else nearby. Choose one object that can fit inside a 5-foot (1.5-meter) cube and that you can see within long range. The object vanishes and appears in your hands or in an open space anywhere you choose within immediate range. Action.

Force Field (3 Intellect points): You create an invisible energy barrier around a creature or object you choose within short range. The force field moves with the creature or object and lasts for ten minutes. The target has +1 to Armor until the effect ends. Action.

Overload Machine (3+ Intellect points): You infuse a powered numenera device of less than level 3 with more energy than it can handle. If affected, the device is destroyed (if an oddity, a cypher, or an artifact) or disabled for at least one minute (if a more substantial machine). The GM may rule that the disabling effect lasts until the device is repaired.

Instead of applying Effort to decrease the difficulty, you can apply Effort to increase the maximum level of the target. Thus, to overload a level 5 device (two levels above the normal limit), you must apply two levels of Effort. Smart nanos use the Machine Interface or Scan esotery on a machine to learn its level before trying to overload it. Action.

Retrieve Memories (3 Intellect points): You touch the remains of a recently slain creature and restore its mind to life long enough to learn information from it. Touch a dead creature and make an Intellect-based roll. The GM sets the difficulty based on the amount of time that has passed since the creature died. A creature that has been dead for only a few minutes is a difficulty 2 task. A creature that has been dead for an hour is a difficulty 4 task. Finally, a creature that has been dead for a few days is a difficulty 9 task. If you succeed on the task, you awaken the corpse, causing its head to animate and perceive things as if it were alive. This enables communication for about one minute, which is about how long it takes for the creature to realize that it's dead.

The creature is limited to what it knew in life, though it cannot recall minor memories, only big events of importance to it. When the effect ends, or if you fail the roll, the creature's brain dissolves to mush and cannot be awakened again. Action.

Reveal (2+ Intellect points): You adjust a creature's eyesight so that it can see normally in areas of dim light and darkness. You can affect one willing creature within immediate range for one hour. Instead of applying Effort to decrease the difficulty of this esotery, you can apply Effort to affect more targets, with each level of Effort affecting two additional targets. You must touch additional targets to affect them. Action to initiate.

Shock to the System (3 Intellect points): You flood the mind of a target within short range with disturbing images and ideas. Affected targets faint and collapse to the ground, remaining unconscious for two rounds (this is instantly negated if they suffer any damage). GMs will modify the difficulty of the roll to affect a target based on logic—it's probably easier to make a shopkeeper faint than a rampaging margr, even if they're both the same level. Action.

Speed Recovery (3 Intellect points): You adjust a creature's normal regenerative ability so that he recovers more quickly. One creature you choose within short range makes a recovery roll without having to spend the time to do so. Action.

THIRD-TIER NANO

Accelerate (4+ Intellect points): You imbue a creature with vitality and energy, allowing it to act more quickly. One willing creature you choose within immediate range accelerates for one minute. The creature has an asset for initiative tasks and Speed defense rolls. Instead of applying Effort to decrease the difficulty of this esotery, you can apply Effort to affect more targets, with each level of Effort affecting one additional target. You must touch additional targets to accelerate them. Action to initiate.

Disassemble (4 Intellect points): You cause an object to rapidly dismantle into ten pieces of equal weight. You must be able to see the object, the object must be your size or smaller, and the object cannot be worn or carried by another creature. The pieces gently fall to the ground around the place where the object stood. Action.

Many nanos develop beneficial esoteries that affect not only themselves but also their companions. These wise innovators know that although it's nice to see in the dark, for example, it's much better if one's allies can also see in the dark. Less responsibility on the nano that way.

Scan, page 36
Margr, page 244

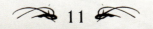

Fabricate Minion (4 Intellect points): You fashion a machinelike minion from raw materials around you. The minion can look like whatever you choose, though the materials you use to create it may limit its appearance. You may assemble the minion anywhere within immediate range. The minion is a level 3 creature of your size or smaller and accompanies you and follows your instructions. As a level 3 creature, it has a target number of 9 and a health of 9, and it inflicts 3 points of damage. The minion moves by walking. A minion remains in your service for one hour or until it is dead. Action to initiate.

Fire and Ice (4 Intellect points): You cause a target within short range to become either very hot or very cold (your choice). If affected, the target suffers 3 points of ambient damage (ignores Armor) each round for up to three rounds, although a new roll is required each round to affect the target. Action to initiate.

Fling (4 Intellect points): Choose a creature or object that is about your size or smaller and within short range. You violently launch it a short distance in any direction you choose. This is an Intellect attack that deals 4 points of damage. Action.

Implant Suggestion (4 Intellect points): You implant a suggestion in the mind of a creature within immediate range. Describe a course of activity to the creature and the conditions under which the creature will perform it. The course of activity must be within the creature's capabilities, and the conditions under which it would perform the activity must be something that directly affects the creature or occurs in its immediate environment. Then make an Intellect attack against that creature. If you succeed, you implant the suggestion, and if the conditions occur within the next 28 hours, the creature does as you suggest. If you attempt to implant a suggestion that would jeopardize the creature's life, livelihood, loved ones, or property, the difficulty of the task is increased by two steps. Action.

Mutation Enhancement (3 Intellect points): You touch a mutant (which may be yourself) and enhance her mutation, if applicable. For the next ten minutes, any time the mutant uses her power(s), she can choose one of the following enhancements:

- All difficulties involved are reduced by one step.

- Range is increased by one category.
- Damaged inflicted is increased by 2 points.

Action.

FOUTH-TIER NANO

Construction (4 Intellect points): You build a structure from nonliving materials drawn from your environment within long range. When the structure appears, it draws up rocks, dirt, scrap metal, and anything else around you to become what you wish it to become. You might create a bridge across a chasm or a shelter where you and your companions can rest. The structure can have any shape you choose and can be big enough to accommodate up to one hundred people. If you create a building, you may divide the interior into as many chambers as you like, though each chamber must have at least one opening. You may also mold the interiors to create rudimentary furniture, such as tables, chairs, and platforms. When you use Construction, it takes ten minutes for the structure to finish taking shape. A structure you create lasts for 28 hours and then collapses into rubble. Action to initiate.

Exile (5 Intellect points): You send a target that you touch hurtling into another random dimension or universe, where it remains for ten minutes. You have no idea what happens to the target while it's gone, but at the end of ten minutes, it returns to the precise spot it left. Action.

Ignition (4 Intellect points): You cause a creature or flammable object you choose within short range to catch fire. You must be able to see the target to affect it. This is an Intellect attack. On a success, the target takes 6 points of damage (ambient damage) per round until the flames are extinguished, which a creature can do by dousing itself in water, rolling around on the ground, or smothering the flames. Usually, putting out the flames takes an action. Action to initiate.

Matter Cloud (5 Intellect points): Pebbles, dirt, sand, and debris rise into the air around you to form a swirling cloud. The cloud extends out to immediate range and moves with you. The cloud remains around you for one minute. When it ends, all the materials fall to the ground around you. The cloud makes it harder for other creatures to attack you. You have an asset on all Speed defense rolls until the effect ends.

In addition, while the cloud is around you,

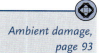

Ambient damage, page 93

GM Intrusion idea for Exile: The exiled target returns but is fully healed or sporting a new weapon, defense, or knowledge gained while in the other universe.

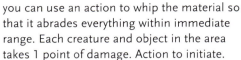

you can use an action to whip the material so that it abrades everything within immediate range. Each creature and object in the area takes 1 point of damage. Action to initiate.

Open (4 Intellect points): You tear apart the defenses of a creature within long range. Any energy-based defenses (such as a force field or a Ward esotery) it has are negated for 1d6 + 1 rounds. If the creature has no energy defenses, its Armor is reduced by 2 for one minute. If it has no energy-based defenses or Armor, the difficulty of all attacks made against the creature is modified by one step to its detriment for one minute. Action.

Projection (4 Intellect points): You project an image of yourself to any location you have seen or previously visited. Distance does not matter as long as the location is on the same world as you. The projection copies your appearance, movements, and any sounds you make for the next ten minutes. Anyone present at the location can see and hear you as if you were there. However, you do not perceive through your projection. Action to initiate.

Wormhole (6 Intellect points): You create a doorway through time and space. The shortcut manifests as a hole in reality large enough to accommodate you and creatures of your size or smaller. One side of the doorway appears anywhere within immediate range, and the other side opens at a spot you choose anywhere within long range. Any character or object moving into one side exits from the other. The door remains open for one minute or until you use an action to close it. Action to initiate.

FIFTH-TIER NANO

Boost Physicality (6 Intellect points): You touch another creature. That creature gains one of the following enhancements of its choice, which lasts for ten minutes:

- Training in all Might tasks and Speed tasks
- +2 Edge in Might and Speed
- 4 additional points of damage

Action.

Concussion (7 Intellect points): You cause a pulse of concussive force to explode out from a point you choose within long range. The pulse extends out in all directions, up to short range. Everything within the pulse's area takes 5 points of damage. Even if you fail the attack roll, targets in the area take 1 point of damage. Action.

Create (7 Intellect points): You create something from nothing. You can create any item you choose that would ordinarily have a difficulty of 5 or less (see the Crafting Items table, page 107 of the corebook). Once created, the item lasts for a number of hours equal to 6 minus the difficulty to create the item. Thus, if you create a glowglobe (difficulty 5), it would last for one hour. Action.

Divide Your Mind (7 Intellect points): You split your consciousness into two parts. For one minute, you can take two actions on each of your turns, but only one of them can be to use an esotery. Action.

Fast Travel (7 Intellect points): You warp time and space so that you and up to ten other creatures within immediate distance travel overland at ten times the normal rate for up to eight hours. At this speed, most

dangerous encounters or regions of rough terrain are ignored, though the GM may declare exceptions. Outright barriers still present a problem. Action to initiate.

Stimulate (6 Intellect points): Touch a target. The difficulty of the next action it takes is decreased by three steps. Action.

SIXTH-TIER NANO

Earthquake (10 Intellect points): You trigger an earthquake centered on a spot you can see within 1,000 feet (305 m). The ground within 250 feet (76 m) of that spot heaves and shakes for five minutes, causing widespread damage to structures and terrain in the area. Buildings made of wood, stone, or brick collapse, walls topple, cliffs crumble, ceilings cave in, some areas of ground rise up, and other areas sink. Characters inside collapsed buildings or beneath a crumbling cliff or falling wall are subject to a crush or a huge crush and may have to dig themselves free, as the GM decides. A crush inflicts 3 points of damage, and a huge crush deals 6 points. Furthermore, the force of the quake is sufficient to knock creatures to the ground and prevent them from standing until the shaking stops. Action to initiate.

Freeze Time (9 Intellect points): You cause time to stop flowing everywhere within immediate range for one minute. The effect immediately ends if you leave the area or if you use an action to end it early. The freezing affects everything in the area except you. Affected creatures are frozen in the moment when you used this esotery, and when the effect ends, they resume what they were doing as if no time had passed. Affected creatures and objects are impervious to all damage and cannot be moved or manipulated. You and everything outside the area act normally. Action to initiate.

Relocate (7 Intellect points): Choose one creature or object within immediate range. You instantly transport it to a new position within long range that you can see. The new position can be any direction from you, but it cannot be inside a solid object. If you succeed on your roll, the target disappears and reappears in its new position. Action.

JACK:
NEW TRICKS OF THE TRADE
Jacks can add these new tricks of the trade into the mix when selecting their tricks of the trade for each tier.

Tricks of the Trade, page 42

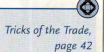

Esoteries are more showy than some of the abilities of other characters, but that doesn't make them better. Just more dramatic. Nanos often have a flair for such things, while glaives and jacks are often more practical.

FIRST-TIER JACK

Combat Ruse (1 Speed point): You feint or juke to mislead your foe and foil its defenses. Choose a creature within short range. If you succeed on a Speed roll, the next character to attack that creature before the end of your next turn has an asset to its attack roll. Action.

Decipher (1 Intellect point): If you spend one minute examining a piece of writing or code in a language you do not understand, you can make an Intellect roll of difficulty 3 (or higher, based on the complexity of the language or code). On a success, you get the gist of what the writing says. Action to initiate.

Gather Rumors (1+ Intellect point): When you spend a few hours in an inhabited urban environment about the size of a town or larger, the GM must tell you one rumor that pertains to the community. Instead of applying Effort to decrease the difficulty, you can apply Effort to learn additional rumors, with each level of Effort revealing one more rumor. Enabler.

Rope Trick: You are trained in all tasks requiring a rope. Further, you can set nonlethal traps with a rope that are one level higher than they would normally be to detect or avoid. Enabler.

Sabotage: You are particularly good at bypassing locks and dismantling devices. You are trained in lockpicking, the numenera, and any task that involves sabotaging an object. Enabler.

Tracer (1 Intellect point): You touch a creature. For the next hour, you know the creature's direction relative to your current position, but you don't know its distance from you. Action to initiate.

Vision: You can see clearly in dim light, very dim light, and darkness. Enabler.

SECOND-TIER JACK

Blackout (2 Intellect points): You cause all light sources within short range—numenera or otherwise—to fade to darkness for ten minutes. Action.

Contortionist (2 Speed points): You can wriggle free from bindings or squeeze through a tight spot. You are trained in escaping. When you use an action to escape or move through a tight area, you can immediately use another action. You may use this action only to move. Enabler.

Crowd Control (3 Intellect points): If you succeed at an Intellect-based deception task, you capture and hold the attention of everyone within 90 feet (27 m) for up to ten minutes.

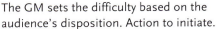

The GM sets the difficulty based on the audience's disposition. Action to initiate.

Erase Memories (3 Intellect points): You reach into a creature's mind to make it forget. Choose one creature within immediate range and make an Intellect roll. On a success, you erase up to the last five minutes of the creature's memory. The creature simply forgets anything it experienced during this time. Action.

Eye for Detail (2 Intellect points): When you spend five minutes or so thoroughly exploring an area no larger than a typical room, you can ask the GM one question about the area. The GM must answer you truthfully. You cannot use this trick of the trade more than one time per area per 28 hours. Enabler.

Far Step (2 Intellect points): You leap through the air and land some distance away. You can jump up, down, or across to anywhere you choose within long range if you have a clear and unobstructed path to that location. You land safely. Action.

Hunker Down (3 Speed points): When you have cover, you have an asset on Speed defense rolls. Enabler.

Opportunist: You have an asset on any attack roll you make against a creature that has been attacked at some point during the round and is within immediate range. Enabler.

Quick Recovery: Your second recovery roll (usually requiring ten minutes) takes only a single action, just like the first roll. Enabler.

Sense Ambush: You are never treated as surprised by an attack. Enabler.

Surprise Strike (3 Speed points): When you attack a creature you have surprised, the difficulty of your attack roll is reduced by one step, and, on a success, you deal 1 additional point of damage. Enabler.

Threaten (3 Intellect points): When you reduce a creature to 0 health, you deliver a vicious threat to another creature within immediate range. Make a Might roll. On a success, the difficulty of all Speed defense rolls made to resist the creature's attacks is reduced by one step until the end of the next round. Enabler.

THIRD-TIER JACK

Controlled Fall: When you fall while you are able to use actions and within reach of a vertical surface, you can attempt to slow your fall. Make a Speed roll. The difficulty is 1 for every 20 feet (6.1 m) you fall. On a success, you take half damage from the fall. If you reduce the difficulty to 0, you take no damage. Enabler.

Gambler: Each day, choose two different numbers from 2 to 16. One number is your lucky number, and the other is your unlucky number. Whenever you make a roll that day and get a number matching your lucky number, the difficulty of your next task is reduced by one step. Whenever you make a roll that day and get a number matching your unlucky number, the difficulty of your next task is increased by one step. Enabler.

Improvise (2 Intellect points): When you perform a task in which you are not trained, you can improvise to gain an asset for the task. The asset might be a tool you cobble together, a sudden insight into overcoming a problem, or a rush of dumb luck. Enabler.

Revelation (3 Intellect points): Choose one of your stats. When you succeed on a task using that stat and you applied at least one level of Effort, the difficulty of the next task you perform within one minute using that stat is reduced by one step. Enabler.

Shock to the System (4 Intellect points): You flood the mind of a target within short range with disturbing images and ideas. Affected targets faint and collapse to the ground, remaining unconscious for two rounds (this is instantly negated if they suffer any damage). GMs will modify the difficulty of the roll to affect a target based on logic—it's probably easier to make a shopkeeper faint than a rampaging margr, even if they're both the same level. Action.

Subterfuge: When you move no more than a short distance, you can move without making a sound, regardless of the surface you move across. Enabler.

Tool Mastery: When you have an asset from using a tool, you reduce the time it takes to perform the task by half (minimum one round). Enabler.

FOURTH-TIER JACK

Ambusher: When you attack a creature that has not yet acted during the first round of combat, the difficulty of your attack is reduced by one step. Enabler.

Confounding Banter (4 Intellect points): You spew a stream of nonsense to distract a foe. Make an Intellect roll against a creature within immediate range. On a success, the difficulty of the defense roll against the creature's next attack before the end of the next round is reduced by one step. Action.

Deadly Aim (4 Speed points): For the next minute, all ranged attacks you make inflict 2 additional points of damage. Action to initiate.

Implant Suggestion (5 Intellect points): You implant a suggestion in the mind of a creature within immediate range. Describe a course of activity to the creature and the conditions under which the creature will perform it. The course of activity must be within the creature's capabilities, and the conditions under which it would perform the activity must be something that directly affects the creature or occurs in its immediate environment. Then make an Intellect attack against that creature. If you succeed, you implant the suggestion, and if the conditions occur within the next 28 hours, the creature does as you suggest. If you attempt to implant a suggestion that would jeopardize the creature's life, livelihood, loved ones, or property, the difficulty of the task is increased by two steps. Action.

Outwit: When you make a Speed defense roll, you can use Intellect in place of your Speed. Enabler.

Preternatural Senses: While you are conscious and able to use an action, you cannot be surprised. In addition, you are trained in initiative actions. Enabler.

Seize Opportunity (5 Speed points): If you succeed on a Speed defense roll to resist an attack, you gain an action. You can use it immediately even if you have already taken a turn in the round. If you use this action to attack, the difficulty of your attack is reduced by one step. You don't take an action during the next round. Enabler.

Tumbling Moves (5 Speed points): When you use an action to move, the difficulty of all Speed defense rolls is reduced by one step until the end of your next turn. Enabler.

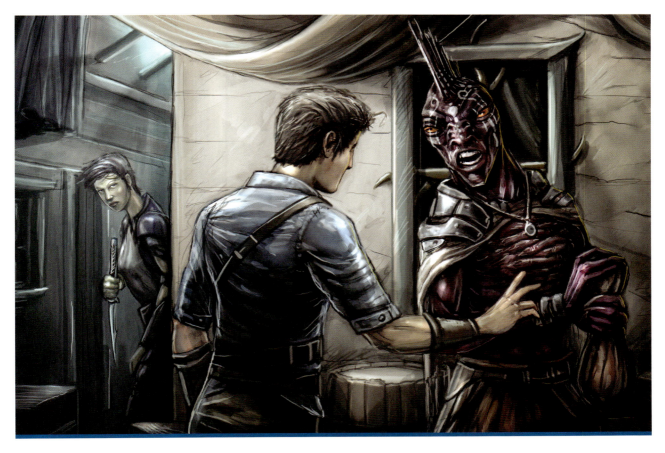

FIFTH-TIER JACK

Mask (5 Intellect points): You transform your body to become someone else. You can change any physical characteristic you wish, including coloration, height, weight, gender, and distinguishing markings. You may also change the appearance of whatever you are wearing or carrying. Your stats, as well as the stats of your items, are unchanged. You remain in this form for up to 28 hours or until you use an action to resume your normal appearance. Action to initiate.

Open (5 Intellect points): You tear apart the defenses of a creature within long range. Any energy-based defenses (such as a force field or a Ward esotery) it has are negated for 1d6 + 1 rounds. If the creature has no energy defenses, its Armor is reduced by 2 for one minute. If it has no energy-based defenses or Armor, the difficulty of all attacks made against the creature is modified by one step to its detriment for one minute. Action.

Uncanny Luck (4 Speed points): When you roll for a task and succeed, you can roll again. If the second number rolled is higher than the first, you get a minor effect. If you roll the same number again, you get a major effect. Enabler.

Vigilant (7 Might points): When you would normally be dazed or stunned, you are not dazed or stunned. Enabler.

SIXTH-TIER JACK

Exploit Advantage: Whenever you roll and you have an asset for that roll, the difficulty is also reduced by one step. Enabler.

Inspiring Success (6 Intellect points): Choose a stat. When you succeed on a roll to perform a task related to that stat and you applied at least one level of Effort, you may choose another PC within short range. That PC has an asset for the next task she attempts using that stat before the end of your next turn. Enabler.

Spring Away (6 Speed points): Whenever you succeed on a Speed defense roll, you can immediately move up to a short distance. You cannot use this ability more than once in a given round. Enabler.

Stimulate (6 Intellect points): Touch a target. The difficulty of the next action it takes is decreased by three steps. Action.

Twist of Fate: When you roll a 1 on the die, you can reroll. You must use the new result, even if it is another 1. Enabler.

DESCRIPTORS

Your descriptor defines your character—it flavors everything you do. The differences between a Cruel glaive and an Honorable glaive are considerable. The descriptor changes the way those characters go about every action. Your descriptor places your character in the situation (the first adventure, which starts the campaign) and helps provide motivation. It is the adjective of the sentence "I am an *adjective noun* who *verbs*."

The descriptors in this chapter are intended to be added to the descriptors in chapter 5 of the Numenera corebook. They offer additional choices for character creation. When added into the mix with the descriptors in the corebook, the racial options (which are really descriptors) in the corebook, and the descriptors found in this book, the choices are indeed many.

Unlike the descriptors in the corebook, some of the descriptors here are negative in connotation. Clumsy, Cruel, Dishonorable, and Hideous, for example, are not terms that most people would want to use to describe themselves. Still, sometimes a character is more accurately defined by something less than flattering. Sometimes this negative trait is the most remarkable one. Like all descriptors, these have been created to help shape a character, and despite their less-than-positive nature, overall, the descriptors are equal in what they offer a character. In other words, the positive aspects of being clumsy make it a "balanced" choice. The point is to have the character you really want to play and have fun without paying a price for doing it.

Descriptors offer a one-time package of extra abilities, skills, or modifications to your stat Pools. Not all of a descriptor's offerings are positive character modifications. For example, some descriptors have inabilities—tasks that a character isn't good at. You can think of inabilities as "negative skills"—instead of being one step better at that kind of task, you're one step worse. If you become skilled at a task that you have an inability with, they cancel out. Remember that characters are defined as much by what they're *not* good at as by what they *are* good at.

Cruel, page 20
Honorable, page 25

Stat Pools, page 20
Descriptors, page 47
Racial options, page 120

Clumsy, page 19
Dishonorable, page 20
Hideous, page 24

GENERAL DESCRIPTORS TABLE

Charming*	Exiled	Intelligent*	Stealthy*
Clever*	Foolish	Learned*	Strong*
Clumsy	Graceful*	Mad	Strong-Willed*
Craven	Guarded	Mystical/Mechanical*	Swift*
Cruel	Hardy	Naive	Tongue-Tied
Dishonorable	Hideous	Noble	Tough*
Doomed	Honorable	Perceptive	Vengeful
Driven	Impulsive	Resilient	Wealthy
Empathic	Inquisitive	Rugged*	Weird

Descriptors marked with asterisks appear in the Numenera corebook.

Descriptors also offer a few brief suggestions of how your character got involved with the rest of the group on the first adventure. You can use these, or not, as you wish.

The general descriptor section offers more than twenty new descriptors, such as Doomed, Naive, Noble, and Tongue-Tied.

The location-based descriptor section covers the nine kingdoms of the Steadfast as well as some options from the Beyond. These include Naven, Ghanic, Draolic, Thaemic, Malvic, Iscobean, Pytharon, Milavian, Ancuani, Ephrem, Bazian, Icebound, and Wasteland.

Last, the racial options section includes four new nonhuman races that you can take as your descriptor: diruk, golthiar, mlox, and nalurus. You can also choose from a selection of new beneficial, harmful, powerful, and distinctive mutations.

You can pick any descriptor you wish regardless of whether you're a glaive, nano, or jack.

GENERAL DESCRIPTORS

CLUMSY

Graceless and awkward, you were told that you'd grow out of it, but you never did. You often drop things, trip over your own feet, or knock things (or people) over. Some people get frustrated by this quality, but most find it funny and even a little charming.

You gain the following characteristics:

Butterfingers: −2 to your Speed Pool.

Thick-Muscled: +2 to your Might Pool.

Inelegant: You have a certain lovable charm. You are trained in all pleasant social interactions when you express a lighthearted, self-deprecating manner.

Dumb Luck: The GM can introduce a GM intrusion on you, based on your clumsiness, without awarding you any XP (as if you had rolled a 1 on a d20 roll). However, if this happens, 50% of the time, your clumsiness works to your advantage. Rather than hurting you (much), it helps, or it hurts your enemies. You slip, but it's just in time to duck an attack. You fall down, but you trip your enemies as you crash into their legs. You turn around too quickly, but you end up knocking the weapon from your foe's hand. You and the GM should work together to determine the details. The GM can use GM intrusions based on your clumsiness normally (awarding XP) if she desires.

Skill: You've got a certain bull-like quality. You are trained in tasks involving breaking things.

Inability: The difficulty of any task that involves balance, grace, or hand-to-eye coordination is increased by one step.

Initial Link to the Starting Adventure: From the following list of options, choose how you became involved in the first adventure.

1. You were in the right place at the right time.

2. You had a piece of information that the other PCs needed to make their plans.

3. A sibling recommended you to the other PCs.

4. You stumbled into the PCs as they were discussing their mission, and they took a liking to you.

CRAVEN

Courage fails you at every turn. You lack the willpower and resolve to stand fast in the face of danger. Fear gnaws at your heart, chewing away at your mind, driving you to distraction until you cannot bear it. Most times, you back down from confrontations. You flee from

Some players won't want to be defined by a "negative" quality like clumsy, but in truth, even this kind of descriptor has enough advantages that it makes for capable and talented characters. What negative descriptors really do is make more interesting and complex characters that are often great fun to play.

threats and vacillate when faced with difficult decisions.

Yet for all that fear dogs you and possibly shames you, your cowardly nature proves to be a useful ally from time to time. Listening to your fears has helped you escape danger and avoid taking unnecessary risks. Others may have suffered in your place, and you might be the first to admit this fact, but secretly you feel intense relief from having avoided an unthinkable and terrible fate.

You gain the following characteristics:

Furtive: +2 to your Speed Pool.

Skill: You're trained in stealth-based tasks.

Skill: You're trained in running actions.

Skill: You're trained in any action made to escape danger, flee from a dangerous situation, or wheedle your way out trouble.

Inability: You do not willingly enter dangerous situations. The difficulty of any initiative actions (to determine who goes first in combat) is increased by one step.

Inability: You fall to pieces when you have to undertake a dangerous task alone. The difficulty of any potentially dangerous task you undertake alone (such as attacking a creature by yourself) is increased by one step.

Additional Equipment: You have a good luck charm or protective device to keep you out of harm's way. You begin the game with one extra oddity.

Initial Link to the Starting Adventure: From the following list of options, choose how you became involved in the first adventure.

1. You believe that you're being hunted, and you have hired one of the other PCs as your protector.

2. You seek to escape your shame and take up with capable individuals in the hopes of repairing your reputation.

3. One of the other PCs bullied you into coming along.

4. The group answered your cries for help when you were in trouble.

CRUEL

Misfortune and suffering do not move you. When another endures hardship, you find it hard to care, and you may even enjoy the pain and difficulty the person experiences. Your cruel streak may derive from bitterness brought about by your own struggles and disappointments. You might be a hard pragmatist, doing what you feel you must even if others are worse for it. Or you could be a sadist, delighting in the pain you inflict.

Being cruel does not necessarily make you a villain. Your cruelty may be reserved for those who cross you or other people useful to you. You might have become cruel as the result of an intensely awful experience. Abuse and torture, for example, can strip away compassion for other living beings.

As well, you need not be cruel in every situation. In fact, others might see you as personable, friendly, and even helpful. But when angered or frustrated, your true nature reveals itself, and those who have earned your scorn are likely to suffer for it.

You gain the following characteristics:

Cunning: +2 to your Intellect Pool.

Cruelty: When you use force, you can choose to maim or deliver painful injuries to draw out your foe's suffering. Whenever you inflict damage, you can choose to inflict 2 fewer points of damage to decrease the difficulty of the next attack against that foe by one step.

Skill: You're trained in tasks related to deception, intimidation, and persuasion when you interact with characters experiencing physical or emotional pain.

Inability: You have a hard time connecting with others, understanding their motives, or sharing their feelings. The difficulty of any task made to ascertain another character's motives, feelings, or disposition is increased by one step.

Additional Equipment: You have a valuable memento from the last person you destroyed. The memento is worth 10 shins, and you can sell it or trade it for an item of equal or lesser value.

Initial Link to the Starting Adventure: From the following list of options, choose how you became involved in the first adventure.

1. You suspect that you might gain a long-term advantage from helping the other PCs and may be able to use that advantage against your enemies.

2. By joining the PCs, you see an opportunity to grow your personal power and status at the expense of others.

3. You hope to make another PC's life more difficult by joining the group.

4. Joining the PCs gives you an opportunity to escape justice for a crime you committed.

DISHONORABLE

There is no honor among thieves—or betrayers, backstabbers, liars, or cheats. You are all of these things, and either you don't

You can pick any descriptor you wish regardless of whether you're a glaive, nano, or jack.

Descriptors like Craven, Cruel, and Dishonorable might not be appropriate for every group. These are villainous traits and some people want their PCs to be entirely heroic. But others don't mind a little "moral greyness" thrown into the mix. Still others see things like Craven and Cruel as traits to overcome as their characters develop (probably earning them different descriptors).

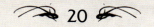

lose any sleep over it, or you deny the truth to others or to yourself. Regardless, you are willing to do whatever it takes to get your own way. Honor, ethics, and principles are merely words. In your estimation, they have no place in the real world.

You gain the following characteristics:

Sneaky: +4 to your Speed Pool.

Just Desserts: When the GM gives another character an XP to award to someone for a GM intrusion, that character cannot give it to you.

Skill: You are trained in deception.

Skill: You are trained in stealth.

Skill: You are trained in intimidation.

Inability: People don't like or trust you. The difficulty of pleasant social interactions is increased by one step.

Initial Link to the Starting Adventure: From the following list of options, choose how you became involved in the first adventure.

1. You are interested in what the PCs are doing, so you lied to them to get into their group.

2. While skulking about, you overheard the PCs' plans and realized that you wanted in.

3. One of the other PCs invited you, having no idea of what you're truly like.

4. You bullied your way in with intimidation and bluster.

DOOMED

You are quite certain that your fate is leading you, inextricably, toward a terrible end. This fate might be yours alone, or you might be dragging along the others closest to you.

You gain the following characteristics:

Jumpy: +2 to your Speed Pool.

Skill: Always on the lookout for danger, you are trained in perception-related tasks.

Skill: You are defense minded, so you are trained in Speed defense tasks.

Skill: You are cynical and expect the worst. Thus, you are resistant to mental shocks. You are trained in Intellect defense tasks having to do with losing your sanity.

Doom: Every other time the GM uses GM intrusion on your character, you cannot refuse it and do not get an XP for it (you still get an XP to award to another player). This is because you are doomed. The universe is a cold, uncaring place, and your efforts are futile at best.

Initial Link to the Starting Adventure: From the following list of options, choose how you became involved in the first adventure.

1. You attempted to avoid it, but events seemed to conspire to draw you to where you are.

2. Why not? It doesn't matter. You're doomed no matter what you do.

3. One of the other PCs saved your life, and now you're repaying that obligation by helping her with the task at hand.

4. You suspect that the only hope you have of avoiding your fate might lie on this path.

DRIVEN

You have set your sights on a goal, and everything you do is in pursuit of that objective. The thing you seek defines you—it shapes your decisions, colors your outlook, and impels you to take action even when

your body and mind scream for you to give up and set the task aside, at least for a while. No matter the hardships you face along the way, you believe in your purpose and will let nothing stop you from achieving it.

When you choose this descriptor, choose a goal that is possible to attain. You might set a goal of finding a lost parent, making a sacrifice at a rumored temple, learning how to perform a particular task, or gaining the funds to pay for a healer to treat a loved one. Once you achieve this goal, you may choose a new one.

You probably talk about your mission all the time, bringing it up even when it's only tangentially connected to the conversation. You usually consider other pursuits in the context of whether or not it advances your own agenda.

You gain the following characteristics:

Determined: +2 to your Might Pool.

Skill: You're trained in Intellect defense actions.

Skill: Each day, choose one skill that you believe will clearly help you reach your goal. You are trained in tasks related to that skill.

Inability: Your commitment to your goals makes it hard to relate to others who don't share your objectives or to notice things that don't pertain to your present mission. The difficulty of all perception tasks is increased by one step.

Initial Link to the Starting Adventure: From the following list of options, choose how you became involved in the first adventure.

1. You saw that the other PCs were pursuing the same goal as you, and you believed that joining forces would improve both of your chances at attaining your objectives.

2. One of the PCs gave you information or other assistance in your mission, and you now repay the favor.

3. Helping the PCs may put key resources you need to complete your mission into your hands.

4. One of the other PCs found you when you were wounded and nursed you back to health.

EMPATHIC

Other people are open books to you. You may have a knack for reading a person's tells, those subtle movements that convey an individual's mood and disposition. Or you may receive information in a more direct way, feeling a person's emotions as if they were tangible things, sensations that lightly brush against

your mind. Your gift for empathy helps you navigate social situations and control them to avoid misunderstandings and prevent useless conflicts from erupting.

The constant bombardment of emotions from those around you likely takes a toll. You might move with the prevailing mood, swinging from giddy happiness to bitter sorrow with little warning. Or you might close yourself off and remain inscrutable to others out of a sense of self-preservation or an unconscious fear that everyone else might learn how you truly feel.

You gain the following characteristics:

Open Mind: +4 to your Intellect Pool.

Skill: You're trained in tasks involving sensing other emotions, discerning dispositions, and getting a hunch about people around you.

Skill: You're trained in all tasks involving social interaction, pleasant or otherwise.

Inability: Being so receptive to others' thoughts and moods makes you vulnerable to anything that attacks your mind. The difficulty of Intellect defense rolls is increased by one step.

Initial Link to the Starting Adventure: From the following list of options, choose how you became involved in the first adventure.

1. You sensed the commitment to the task the other PCs have and felt moved to help them.

2. You established a close bond with another PC and can't bear to be parted from him or her.

3. You sensed something strange in one of the PCs and decided to join the group to see if you can sense it again and uncover the truth.

4. You join the PCs to escape an unpleasant relationship or negative environment.

EXILED

You have walked a long and lonely road, leaving your home and your life behind. You might have committed a heinous crime, something so awful that your people forced you out, and if you dare return, you face death. You might have been accused of a crime you didn't commit and now must pay the price for someone else's wicked deed. Your exile might be the result of a social gaffe—perhaps you shamed your family or a friend, or you embarrassed yourself in front of your peers, an authority, or someone you respect. Whatever the reason, you have left your old life behind and now strive to make a new one.

Driven characters can be "one-note" in some respect, and that can be dull. Some people may want to use Driven as a temporary descriptor that lasts until their mission is done, then choose a different descriptor (see page 89).

You probably have a memento from your past—an old picture, a locket with a few strands of hair inside, or a lighter given to you by someone important. You keep the object close at hand and pull it out to help you remember better times.

You gain the following characteristics:

Self-Reliant: +2 to your Might Pool.

Loner: You gain no benefit when you get help with a task from another character who is trained or specialized in that task.

Skill: You're trained in all tasks involving sneaking.

Skill: You're trained in all tasks involving foraging, hunting, and finding safe places to rest or hide.

Inability: Living on your own for as long as you have makes you slow to trust others and awkward in social situations. The difficulty of any task involving social interactions is increased by one step.

Initial Link to the Starting Adventure: From the following list of options, choose how you became involved in the first adventure.

1. The other PCs earned your trust by helping you when you were in need. You accompany them to repay their aid.

2. While exploring on your own, you discovered something strange. When you traveled to a settlement, the PCs were the only ones who believed you, and they have accompanied you to help you deal with the problem.

3. One of the other PCs reminds you of someone you used to know.

4. You have grown weary of your isolation. Joining the other PCs gives you a chance to belong.

FOOLISH

Not everyone can be brilliant. Oh, you don't think of yourself as stupid, and you're not. It's just that others might have a bit more... wisdom. Insight. You prefer to barrel along headfirst through life and let other people worry about things. Worrying's never helped you, so why bother? You take things at face value and don't fret about what tomorrow might bring.

People call you "idiot" or "numbskull," but it doesn't faze you much.

You gain the following characteristics:

Unwise: –4 to your Intellect Pool.

Carefree: You succeed more on luck than anything. Every time you roll for a task, roll twice and take the higher result.

Intellect Weakness: Any time you spend points from your Intellect Pool, it costs you 1 more point than usual.

Inability: The difficulty of any Intellect defense task is increased by one step.

Inability: The difficulty of any task that involves seeing through a deception, an illusion, or a trap is increased by one step.

Initial Link to the Starting Adventure: From the following list of options, choose how you became involved in the first adventure.

1. Who knows? Seemed like a good idea at the time.

2. Someone asked you to join up with the other PCs. They told you not to ask too many questions, and that seemed fine to you.

3. Your parent (or a parental/mentor figure) got you involved to give you something to do and maybe "teach you some sense."

4. The other PCs needed some muscle that wouldn't overthink things.

GUARDED

You conceal your true nature behind a mask and are loath to let anyone see who you really are. Protecting yourself, physically and emotionally, is what you care about most, and you prefer to keep everyone else at a safe distance. You may be suspicious of everyone you meet, expecting the worst from people so you won't be surprised when they prove you right. Or you might just be a bit reserved, careful about letting people through your gruff exterior to the person you really are.

No one can be as reserved as you are and make many friends. Most likely, you have an abrasive personality and tend to be pessimistic in your outlook. You probably nurse an old hurt and find that the only way you can cope is to keep it and your personality locked down.

You gain the following characteristics:

Suspicious: +2 to your Intellect Pool.

Skill: You are trained in all Intellect defense tasks.

Skill: You are trained in all tasks involving discerning the truth, piercing disguises, and recognizing falsehoods and other deceptions.

Inability: Your suspicious nature makes you unlikeable. The difficulty of any task involving deception or persuasion is increased by one step.

Initial Link to the Starting Adventure: From the following list of options, choose how you became involved in the first adventure.

Weakness, page 118

It can be liberating and really fun to play a foolish character. In some ways, the pressure to always do the right, smart thing is off.

On the other hand, if you play such a character as a bumbling moron in every single situation, that can become annoying to everyone else at the table. As with everything, moderation is the key.

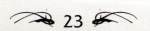

Damage Track,
page 93

1. One of the PCs managed to overcome your defenses and befriend you.

2. You want to see what the PCs are up to, so you accompany them to catch them in the act of some wrongdoing.

3. You have made a few enemies and take up with the PCs for protection.

4. The PCs are the only people who will put up with you.

HARDY

Your body was built to take abuse. Whether you're pounding down stiff drinks while holding up a bar in your favorite watering hole or trading blows with a thug in a back alley, you keep going, shrugging off hurts and injuries that might slow or incapacitate a lesser person. Neither hunger nor thirst, cut flesh nor broken bone can stop you. You just press on through the pain and continue.

As fit and healthy as you are, the signs of wear show in the myriad scars crisscrossing your body, your thrice-broken nose, your cauliflower ears, and any number of other

disfigurements you wear with pride.

You gain the following characteristics:

Mighty: +4 to your Might Pool.

Fast Healer: You halve the time it takes to make a recovery roll (minimum one action).

Unstoppable: While you are impaired, you function as if you were hale. While you are debilitated, you function as if you were impaired. In other words, you don't suffer the effects of being impaired until you become debilitated, and you never suffer the effects of being debilitated. You still die if all your stat Pools are 0.

Skill: You are trained in Might defense actions.

Inability: Your big, strong body is slow to react. The difficulty of any task involving initiative is increased by one step.

Ponderous: When you apply Effort when making a Speed roll, you must spend 1 extra point from your Speed Pool.

Initial Link to the Starting Adventure: From the following list of options, choose how you became involved in the first adventure.

1. The PCs recruited you after learning about your reputation as a survivor.

2. You join the PCs because you want or need the money.

3. The PCs offer you a challenge equal to your physical power.

4. You believe the only way the PCs will succeed is if you are along to protect them.

HIDEOUS

You are physically repugnant by almost any human standard. You might have had a serious accident, a harmful mutation, or just poor genetic luck, but you are incontrovertibly ugly.

You've more than made up for your appearance in other ways, however. Because you had to hide your appearance, you excel at sneaking about unnoticed or disguising yourself. But perhaps most important, being ostracized while others socialized, you took the time growing up to develop yourself as you saw fit—you grew strong or quick, or you honed your mind.

You gain the following characteristics:

Versatile: You get 4 additional points to divide among your stat Pools.

Skill: You are trained in intimidation and any other fear-based interactions.

Skill: You are trained in disguise and stealth tasks.

Inability: The difficulty of all tasks relating

to pleasant social interaction is increased by one step.

Initial Link to the Starting Adventure: From the following list of options, choose how you became involved in the first adventure.

1. One of the other PCs approached you while you were in disguise, recruiting you while believing you were someone else.

2. While skulking about, you overheard the other PCs' plans and realized you wanted in.

3. One of the other PCs invited you, but you wonder if it was out of pity.

4. You bullied your way in with intimidation and bluster.

HONORABLE

You are trustworthy, fair, and forthright. You try to do what is right, to help others, and to treat them well. Lying and cheating are no way to get ahead—these things are for the weak, the lazy, or the despicable. You probably spend a lot of time thinking about your personal honor, how best to maintain it, and how to defend it if challenged. In combat, you are straightforward and offer quarter to any foe. You were likely instilled with this sense of honor by a parent or a mentor. Sometimes the distinction between what is and isn't honorable varies with different schools of thought, but in broad strokes, honorable people can agree on most aspects of what honor means.

You gain the following characteristics:

Stalwart: +2 to your Might Pool.

Skill: You are trained in pleasant social interactions.

Skill: You are trained in discerning people's true motives or seeing through lies.

Initial Link to the Starting Adventure: From the following list of options, choose how you became involved in the first adventure.

1. The PCs' goals appear to be honorable and commendable.

2. You see that what the other PCs are about to do is dangerous, and you'd like to help protect them.

3. One of the other PCs invited you, hearing of your trustworthiness.

4. You asked politely if you could join the other PCs in their mission.

IMPULSIVE

You have a hard time tamping down your enthusiasm. Why wait when you can just do it (whatever it is) and get it done? You deal with problems when they arise rather than

plan ahead. Putting out the small fires now prevents them from becoming one big fire later. You are the first to take risks, to jump in and lend a hand, to step into dark passages, and to find danger.

Your impulsiveness likely gets you into trouble. While others might take time to study the numenera they discover, you use such items without hesitation. After all, the best way to learn what something can do is to use it. When a cautious explorer might look around and check for danger nearby, you have to physically stop yourself from bulling on ahead. Why fuss around when the exciting thing is just ahead?

You gain the following characteristics:

Reckless: +2 to your Speed Pool.

Skill: You're trained in initiative actions (to determine who goes first in combat).

Skill: You're trained in Speed defense actions.

Inability: You'll try anything once or twice. The difficulty of any task that involves patience, willpower, or discipline is increased by one step.

Initial Link to the Starting Adventure: From the following list of options, choose how you became involved in the first adventure.

1. You heard what the other PCs were up to and suddenly decided to join them.

2. You pulled everyone together after you heard rumors about something interesting you want to see or do.

3. You blew all of your money and now find yourself strapped for cash.

4. You're in trouble for acting recklessly. You join the other PCs because they offer a way out of your problem.

INQUISITIVE

The world is vast and mysterious, with wonders and secrets to keep you amazed for several lifetimes. You feel the tugging on your heart, the call to explore the wreckage of past civilizations, to discover new peoples, new places, and whatever bizarre wonders you might find along the way. However, as strongly as you feel the pull to roam the world, you know there is danger aplenty, and you take precautions to ensure that you are prepared for any eventuality. Research, preparation, and readiness will help you live long enough to see everything you want to see and do everything you want to do.

You probably have a dozen books and travelogues about the world on you at any

Impulsive characters get into trouble. That's their thing, and that's fine. But if you're constantly dragging your fellow PCs into trouble (or worse, getting them seriously hurt or killed), that will be annoying, to say the least. A good rule of thumb is that impulsiveness doesn't always mean a predilection to do the wrong thing. Sometimes it's the urge to do the right thing.

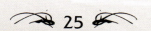

time. When not hitting the road and looking around, you spend your time with your nose in a book, learning everything you can about the place you're going so you know what to expect when you get there.

You gain the following characteristics:

Smart: +4 to your Intellect Pool.

Skill: You are eager to learn. You are trained in any task that involves learning something new, whether you're talking to a local to get information or digging through old books to find lore.

Skill: You have made a study of the world. You are trained in any task involving geography or history.

Inability: You tend to fixate on the details, making you somewhat oblivious to what's going on around you. The difficulty of any task to hear or notice dangers around you is increased by one step.

Inability: When you see something interesting, you hesitate as you take in all the details. The difficulty of initiative actions (to determine who goes first in combat) is increased by one step.

Additional Equipment: You have three books on whatever subjects you choose.

Initial Link to the Starting Adventure: From

the following list of options, choose how you became involved in the first adventure.

1. One of the PCs approached you to learn information related to the mission, having heard you were an expert.

2. You have always wanted to see the place where the other PCs are going.

3. You were interested in what the other PCs were up to and decided to go along with them.

4. One of the PCs fascinates you, perhaps due to a special or weird ability she has.

MAD

You have delved too deeply into subjects humans of the Ninth World were not meant to know. You are knowledgeable in things beyond the scope of most, but this knowledge has come at a terrible price. You are likely in questionable physical shape and occasionally shake with nervous tics. You sometimes mutter to yourself without realizing it.

You gain the following characteristics:

Knowledgeable: +4 to your Intellect Pool.

Fits of Insight: Whenever such knowledge is appropriate, the GM feeds you information although there is no clear explanation as to how you could know such a thing. This is up to the GM's discretion, but it should happen as often as once each session.

Erratic Behavior: You are prone to acting erratically or irrationally. When you are in the presence of a major numenera discovery or subjected to great stress (such as a serious physical threat), the GM can use GM intrusion that directs your next action *without awarding XP*. You can still pay 1 XP to refuse the intrusion. The GM's influence is the manifestation of your madness and thus is always something you would not likely do otherwise, but it is not directly, obviously harmful to you unless there are extenuating circumstances. (For example, if a foe suddenly leaps out of the darkness, you might spend the first round babbling incoherently or screaming the name of your first true love.)

Skill: You are trained in numenera knowledge.

Inability: Your mind is quite fragile. Whenever you try to resist a mental attack, the difficulty is increased by one step.

Initial Link to the Starting Adventure: From the following list of options, choose how you became involved in the first adventure.

1. Voices in your head told you to go.

2. You instigated the whole thing and

convinced the others to join you.

3. One of the other PCs obtained a book of numenera knowledge for you, and now you're repaying that favor by helping her with the task at hand.

4. You feel compelled by inexplicable intuition.

NAIVE

You've lived a sheltered life. Your childhood was safe and secure, so you didn't get a chance to learn much about the world—and even less chance to experience it. Whether you were training for something, had your nose in a book, or just were sequestered in a secluded place, you haven't done much, met many people, or seen many interesting things so far. That's probably going to change soon, but as you go forward into a larger world, you do so without some of the understanding that others possess about how it all works.

You gain the following characteristics:

Fresh: You add +1 to your recovery rolls.

Incorruptible: You are trained in Intellect defense tasks and all tasks that involve resisting temptation.

Skill: You're wide-eyed. You are trained in perception tasks.

Inability: The difficulty of any task that involves seeing through deceptions or determining someone's secret motive is increased by one step.

Initial Link to the Starting Adventure: From the following list of options, choose how you became involved in the first adventure.

1. Someone told you that you should get involved.

2. You needed money, and this seemed like a good way to earn some.

3. You believed that you could learn a lot by joining the other PCs.

4. Sounded like fun.

NOBLE

You are of noble birth. You are not of the common people. Your family has a title and the prestige and (probably) the wealth that goes along with it.

The Ninth World is, generally speaking, a classist place, and in that structure you are in the top echelon. Often, laws don't apply to you, you gain special treatment, and sometimes people do as you command. You probably dress in finery and walk with a noble bearing, but sometimes the nobility

must conceal their station to keep themselves safe—from brigands, thieves, or aristocratic enemies and their servants.

You gain the following characteristics:

Respect: People who are not of noble station often treat you with deference. A few, however, secretly treat you with contempt. The difficulty of interactions with non-nobles is decreased by one step 75% of the time, and increased by one step 25% of the time.

Retainer or Mount: You start with a level 2 servant or mount that serves you faithfully. You and the GM should work out the details.

Contact: You have a contact among the nobility who helps you and treats you well. You and the GM should work out the details.

Skill: You are trained in etiquette and

interacting with the nobility.

Additional Equipment: You begin the game with 20 extra shins and an extra oddity.

Initial Link to the Starting Adventure: From the following list of options, choose how you became involved in the first adventure.

1. It seemed like a lark.

2. You're on the run from an enemy, and joining the PCs seemed like a good way to hide among the common folk.

3. The mission involves somehow redeeming or helping your family.

4. Your parent(s) forced you into it, hoping the experience would be good for you.

PERCEPTIVE

You miss little. You pick out the small details in the world around you and are skilled at making deductions from the information you find. Your talents make you an exceptional sleuth, a formidable scientist, or a talented scout.

As adept as you are at finding clues, you have no skill at picking up on social cues. You overlook an offense that your deductions give or how uncomfortable your scrutiny can make the people around you. You tend to dismiss others as being intellectual dwarfs compared to you, which avails you little when you need a favor.

You gain the following characteristics:

Smart: +2 to your Intellect Pool.

Skill: You have an eye for detail. You are trained in any task that involves finding or noticing small details.

Skill: You know a little about everything. You are trained in any task that involves identifying objects or calling to mind a minor detail or bit of trivia.

Skill: Your skill at making deductions can be imposing. You are trained in any task that involves intimidating another creature.

Inability: Your confidence comes off as arrogance to people who don't know you. The difficulty of any task involving positive social interactions is increased by one step.

Additional Equipment: You have a bag of light tools.

Initial Link to the Starting Adventure: From the following list of options, choose how you became involved in the first adventure.

1. You overheard the other PCs discussing their mission and volunteered your services.

2. One of the PCs asked you to come along, believing that your talents would be invaluable to the mission.

3. You believe that the PCs' mission is somehow related to one of your investigations.

4. A third party recruited you to follow the PCs and see what they were up to.

RESILIENT

You can take a lot of punishment, both physically and mentally, and still come back for more. It takes a lot to put you down. Neither physical nor mental shocks or damage have a lasting effect. You're tough to faze. Unflappable. Unstoppable.

You gain the following characteristics:

Resistant: +2 to your Might Pool, and +2 to your Intellect Pool.

Recover: You can make an extra recovery roll each day. This roll is just one action. So you can make two recovery rolls that each take one action, one roll that takes ten minutes, a fourth roll that takes one hour, and a fifth roll that requires ten hours of rest.

Skill: You are trained in Might defense tasks.

Skill: You are trained in Intellect defense tasks.

Inability: You're hardy but not necessarily strong. The difficulty of any task involving moving, bending, or breaking things is increased by one step.

Inability: You have a lot of willpower and mental fortitude, but you're not necessarily smart. The difficulty of any task involving knowledge or figuring out problems or puzzles is increased by one step.

Initial Link to the Starting Adventure: From the following list of options, choose how you became involved in the first adventure.

1. You saw that the PCs clearly need someone like you to help them out.

2. Someone asked you to watch over one of the PCs in particular, and you agreed.

3. You are bored and desperately in need of a challenge.

4. You lost a bet—unfairly, you think—and had to take someone's place on this mission.

TONGUE-TIED

You've never been much of a talker. When forced to interact with others, you never think of the right thing to say—words fail you entirely, or they come out all wrong. You often end up saying precisely the wrong thing and insult someone unintentionally. Most of the time, you just keep mum.

This makes you a listener instead—a careful observer. It also means that you're better at

Is there really much difference between a character who is Tough, one who is Hardy, and another who is Resilient? They are indeed close, but the differences will become apparent in play. Players should choose the one they like best.

doing things than talking about them. You're quick to take action.

You gain the following characteristics:

Actions, Not Words: +2 to your Might Pool, and +2 to your Speed Pool.

Skill: You are trained in perception.

Skill: You are trained in initiative (unless it's a social situation).

Inability: The difficulty of all tasks relating to social interaction is increased by one step.

Inability: The difficulty of all tasks involving verbal communication or relaying information is increased by one step.

Initial Link to the Starting Adventure: From the following list of options, choose how you became involved in the first adventure.

1. You just tagged along and no one told you to leave.

2. You saw something important the other PCs did not and (with some effort) managed to relate it to them.

3. You intervened to save one of the other PCs when he was in danger.

4. One of the other PCs recruited you for your talents.

VENGEFUL

One moment changed everything for you. One dreadful encounter, one betrayal, or one horrific tragedy altered your course and made you who you are today. Looking back at that time, you often wonder how your life would have unfolded if not for the event that ruined everything. The life you imagine you should have had haunts you and feeds your appetite for revenge until vengeance is the only thing you have left.

To be vengeful, you must have someone or something you want revenge against and someone or something to avenge. Work with your GM to determine what happened that affected you so strongly. Maybe a group of bandits wiped out your family. A corrupt official stole your family's savings or otherwise brought ruin to you and your loved ones. Perhaps a rival destroyed your romance by sullying your name. Death, finances, love: any of these can support your motivation.

In addition, consider to what extent your character will go to gain vengeance. Will you compromise your values to destroy the ones who wronged you? Will you sacrifice your companions to get what you want? Can you imagine a life after you get revenge, or will you throw yours away to punish the people who wronged you?

You gain the following characteristics:

Skill: The fires of your hatred make you an imposing figure. You're trained in any task that involves intimidation, threats, or inflicting pain through torture.

Skill: You will follow your enemies to the ends of the earth. You're trained in any task that involves finding and following tracks.

Skill: You're trained in Speed defense actions.

Additional Equipment: You have an additional medium weapon.

Initial Link to the Starting Adventure: From the following list of options, choose how you became involved in the first adventure.

1. You and the other PCs are headed in the same direction.

2. You believe that one of the PCs knows something about your enemy. You accompany the group to find out what that character knows.

3. One of the PCs survived the event that caused you to become vengeful. You travel with that character to protect him or her.

4. You drew everyone together to help you get revenge on your enemies.

WEALTHY

You can't remember a time when you wanted for anything. You have always had money and have largely lived a life of comfort and plenty. You might be stingy with your wealth, hiding your abundance lest others try to steal it from you. Or you might be magnanimous, spreading it around to any and all who need it.

The source of your funds is up to you. Maybe you inherited your vast fortune from a relative. A sudden windfall could have made you flush with funds and given you a life you never dreamed of. You might be a successful merchant or entrepreneur, making your fortune through hard work and determination.

You gain the following characteristics:

Connected: You have connections, resources, and a head for business. Whenever you spend at least an hour in a community with a population of 1,000 or more, you can find comfortable accommodations for you and your companions for as long as you stay there. The accommodations also provide you with food and 50 shins to spend in whatever manner you choose.

Skill: You have disposable income. You are trained in any task where having money would be an advantage.

Additional Equipment: You have 50 shins.

Initial Link to the Starting Adventure: From the following list of options, choose how you became involved in the first adventure.

1. You crave a life of adventure. You hired all the other PCs for your expedition.

2. Having wealth only creates an appetite for more. You join the other PCs to grow your fortunes.

3. You want to do good works with your wealth, and you see the PCs' mission as an opportunity to help people.

4. The source of your wealth—a relative, a business, or your position in the community—controls your life, and you have begun to feel stifled. You disguise your true identity and accompany the PCs for a chance at the freedom your fortune denies you.

WEIRD

You aren't like anyone else, and that's fine with you. People don't seem to understand you—they even seem put off by you—but who cares? You understand the Ninth World better than they do because you're weird, and so is the world you live in. The concept of "the weird" is well known to you. Strange devices, ancient locales, bizarre creatures, storms that can transform you, living energy fields, and things most people can't even name populate the world, and you thrive on it. You have a special attachment to it all, and the more you discover about the weirdness in the world, the more you might discover about yourself.

Weird characters might be mutants or born with strange qualities, but sometimes they started out "normal" and adopted the weird by choice.

You gain the following characteristics:

Inner Light: +2 to your Intellect Pool.

Distinctive Physical Quirk: You have a unique physical aspect that is, well, bizarre. For example, perhaps instead of hair, you have metal spikes on your head. Perhaps your hands don't connect to your arms, although they move as if they do. Maybe a third eye stares out from the side of your head, superfluous tendrils grow from your back, or you have no nose. Whatever it is, your quirk might be a mutation, a biomechanical transformation, or a feature with no explanation.

A Sense for the Weird: Sometimes—at the GM's discretion—weird things relating to the numenera or its effects on the world seem to call out to you. You can sense them from afar, and if you get within long range of such a thing, you can sense whether it is overtly dangerous or not.

Skill: You are trained in numenera knowledge.

Inability: People find you unnerving. The difficulty of all tasks relating to pleasant social interaction is increased by one step.

Initial Link to the Starting Adventure: From the following list of options, choose how you became involved in the first adventure.

1. It seemed weird, so why not?

2. Whether the other PCs realize it or not, their mission has to do with something weird that you know about, so you got involved.

3. As an expert in the weird, you were specifically recruited by the other PCs.

4. You felt drawn to join the other PCs, but you don't know why.

From a certain perspective, almost all Numenera characters are weird. So a character with the Weird descriptor really has to go the extra step. Work with the GM to come up with ways to really make your weird character memorable. Remember, though, weird doesn't mean insane or evil. In fact, if Numenera teaches us anything, it's that weird is good.

LOCATION-BASED DESCRIPTORS

These location-based descriptors are provided as an option for characters who are firmly connected to their homeland (or to another place that strongly calls to them for some other reason). Sometimes these connections are to the land itself, other times to the political sensibilities of a place, and still other times to the cultural norms in which a character was raised.

Whether the relationship between the character and the locale is positive or negative, the connection pulls at the PC, largely defining who she is. Not everyone from an area has these characteristics—in fact, having such strong ties to a place is unusual—but those who do embody the very essence of a place in their skills, mindset, and actions.

The descriptors here include one for each land of the Steadfast, followed by a selection from the Beyond.

THE STEADFAST

NAVEN

You think money is the be-all and end-all of the world. Whether you hoard it for your own gain, disperse it among those who need it, or endeavor to run a highly successful business, your mind works a kind of money magic, turning everything you touch into shins. Perhaps this ability comes from being raised among successful money-mongers in the kingdom of Navarene, perhaps it's a genetic skill woven into your blood, or perhaps you've trained hard to improve your business acumen.

You may show off your wealth in the cut and fabric of your clothing or hide it behind a cloak of destitution. Most people like you and are eager to broker deals, but occasionally you run

LOCATION-BASED DESCRIPTORS TABLE		
Naven	Iscobean	Bazian
Ghanic	Pytharon	Icebound
Draolic	Milavian	Wasteland
Thaemic	Ancuani	
Malvic	Ephrem	

across someone who finds you shallow and untrustworthy.

You gain the following characteristics:

Capitalistic: +2 to your Intellect Pool.

Bartering: It's almost as though no one wants to part your money from you. Maybe it's your great smile, your kind word about the stock, or that little bit of fear you instill in the seller. Either way, you always pay half price for goods or services.

Skill: You are trained in all tasks involving the exchange of money.

Skill: You are trained in studying and retaining knowledge of numbers, patterns, and other minute details.

Inability: Although you can defend yourself when necessary, you have never been very good at physical actions. The difficulty of any task involving climbing, jumping, running, or swimming is increased by one step.

Additional Equipment: You have a small box that looks like a book but opens only for the press of your right index finger. This box currently holds an additional 15 shins.

Initial Link to the Starting Adventure: From the following list of options, choose how you became involved in the first adventure.

1. There is a reward involved, and you want the money.

2. You believe there is a business opportunity to be had, and you want to be the one to have it.

3. One of the NPCs involved owes you money for a business deal gone bad, and you intend to get it back.

4. A family that you're close to is desperately in need of some additional money, and you've vowed to help them out.

For additional details on the areas that the location-based descriptors are built on, see the Numenera corebook, Part 4: The Setting.

Navarene, page 137

GHANIC

The Sea Kingdom of Ghan, page 145

The sea—how it calls to you. You can hear it in your blood and feel it in your heart, but your relationship with it is complicated. Perhaps you have run from its constant whisper in your ear, or perhaps you ache to return to it but cannot. Whether you love the sea or despise it, however, it's clearly a part of you. Thanks to your connection with the Sea Kingdom of Ghan, you have an innate knowledge of the water's comings and goings, even when you are far from it, and its rhythms color your patterns of speech and movements.

Even if you don't mean it to, the sea shows up in your clothing choices. You often wear blues and silvers, perhaps with a splash of yellow that appears like sun reflecting off the water's surface. You may have a hat that is designed to protect you from sun, waves, and wind.

You gain the following characteristics:

Contact: You have many friends in watery places. One of your close contacts holds a high-ranking position in Ghan's merchant fleet.

Skill: You're trained in all tasks involving swimming, fishing, or fighting in water.

Skill: You're trained in all tasks involving boats or watercraft of any kind.

Skill: You're trained in navigating by the stars. At night, the difficulty of any task involving navigation or map reading is decreased by one step.

Inability: Something about dry land makes you feel slightly off kilter. The difficulty of all Speed-related tasks on dry land is increased by one step.

Additional Equipment: You have a small egg-shaped item that always smells of sea salt. When held in your right palm, the narrow end points the way to the nearest shore. When held in your left, it points the way toward the nearest fresh water.

Initial Link to the Starting Adventure: From the following list of options, choose how you became involved in the first adventure.

1. One of the other PCs asked you to come along because of your knowledge of the sea.

2. You are on a secret assignment for Ghan's merchant fleet, and this adventure coincides with your mission.

3. You want to prove to yourself that you don't need to heed the sea's call, and you think this might be a good first step.

4. You need money to repair or purchase the boat of your dreams so you can live out the rest of your days on the sea.

DRAOLIC

Living under the banner of the tiger of Draolis has taught you, above all, the power of glory. You believe it can be wielded to vanquish all evil, destroy all enemies, and heal all wounds. For you, recognition isn't the point—it's the means to an end. You don't need all the glory for yourself, either. As long as you garner the lion's share of the accolades and can use them to reach your goal, you're happy to share the attention.

Powerful and captivating, your actions or voice draw all eyes. You likely dress with care, attention, and just the right amount of flair. You probably keep all of your equipment in meticulous shape, your bags are organized, and you're always at the ready to heed a public call to action. You may have a favorite phrase or two that you proclaim at opportune times, usually when all eyes are on you.

You gain the following characteristics:

Intriguing: +4 to your Intellect Pool.

Skill: You're trained in all tasks that have the potential to bring you eminence. This includes competitions, feats of strength or combat, speeches, and other actions that catch the eye of others.

Inability: Sometimes your fierce desire for prestige means you act before you think. The difficulty of all tasks requiring perception, identification, or assessing danger is increased by one step.

Additional Equipment: You carry a carefully folded and very old flag that bears the forbidden tiger symbology of Draolis.

Initial Link to the Starting Adventure: From the following list of options, choose how you became involved in the first adventure.

1. You saw the chance to receive accolades for a job well done and sway the path of someone's thinking.

2. You believe this task plays into your larger plan to bring Draolis back to its former glory.

3. One of the other PCs praised you on a job well done, and you saw the chance to show off your skills.

4. You saw that the PCs were in danger and agreed to help, despite the fact that you're not likely to receive any prestige by doing so.

THAEMIC

Your time in Thaemor has taught you one thing: even the weakest of nations can one day become great. In every thing, great or small, you see the power of potential. The smallest acorn can become a towering tree—but even more than that, the tree can then become part of the finest fence, which can become part of the finest kingdom. Your view is long and grand, and you spend your life making connections between a tiny action and its greatest consequence, between a person and her long-term potential, between a thing and its eventual promise. With the right care and attention, all things (even you) can become something amazing.

It's possible that you prefer your social and cultural footprint to be small in an effort to minimize your long-term effect on the world. Or perhaps you want to change everything, and thus you act with aplomb and carelessness. Some people may find you moving—perhaps even consider you to be a life coach or a futureteller—but others may find your blind optimism about the future irritating at best.

You gain the following characteristics:

Uplifted: +4 to your Intellect Pool.

Skill: It's easy for you to show others their great promise—or their utter lack of it. You are trained in any task involving persuasion, sensing emotions, or getting a hunch about people around you.

Skill: Every object that comes in contact with you has the possibility of being useful. You're trained in any tasks involving crafting.

Idealistic: Your optimism about everything comes with a price. When things don't go as expected, you suffer great doubts that can hinder you. When any member of your party

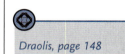

Draolis, page 148

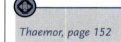

Thaemor, page 152

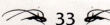

NUMENERA

is impaired, the difficulty of every task you attempt is increased by one step.

Additional Equipment: You have a journal in which you record the patterns and connections that you have noticed throughout your life.

Initial Link to the Starting Adventure: From the following list of options, choose how you became involved in the first adventure.

1. You saw great potential in one of the PCs, and you want to help her achieve it.

2. Your ability to see the long-term consequences of an action made you believe that joining the group would have positive ripple effects.

3. One of the PCs carries an object that will become part of something much greater, and you want to watch it happen.

4. You helped one of the PCs believe in his potential enough to get this job, and he asked you to join them.

MALVIC

Malevich, page 154

Justice and mercy. Justice and mercy. You must have heard that phrase a thousand times in Malevich over the years. When you were younger, you despised the sound of it, having learned that it was all meaningless, thanks to a run-in with the brutal guards known as the Thyrn and their dual swords.

Iscobal, page 158
Queen Whenith
Sarromere, page 158

Now that you're older, you understand the true meaning of the words, and you have dedicated your life to them. You seek to right injustices and teach perpetrators the errors of their way through words and kindness. However, as a product of your upbringing, you can't always shake your violent, harsh nature. If you feel that someone is oppressed, it nearly brings you to fits of rage. You use that power, telling yourself that you're doing it for the good of the world.

Two colors you probably stay away from are black and gold, as they remind you of the Thyrn. Swords, too, are problematic—you may choose to forgo them, or perhaps they are

your weapon of choice, a constant reminder of your purpose.

You gain the following characteristics:

Just: +4 to your Might Pool.

Skill: Nothing gets past you. You are trained in seeing through lies, deception, and disguise.

Skill: You are passionate about your purpose, so much so that you don't even feel the pain of a shattering blow or the sting of a knife slice. You are trained in Might defense tasks.

Inability: You have a hard time trusting people to do what's right, and they sense your constant scrutiny and suspicions. The difficulty of any task involving deception or persuasion is increased by one step.

Additional Equipment: You have a numenera-based tattoo somewhere on your body that says "Justice & Mercy" in some form. The ink sometimes glows red from your skin.

Initial Link to the Starting Adventure: From the following list of options, choose how you became involved in the first adventure.

1. You saw great injustice and know that you're the one to help set things right.

2. You have a plan for revenge upon the Thyrn, and this will bring you one step closer to your goal.

3. You believe in the PCs' cause.

4. One of the PCs shares your desire for justice and invited you to come along.

ISCOBEAN

When you were little, you spent a great deal of time with someone whose job it had been to collect numenera items for Queen Whenith Sarromere of Iscobal. That person told you all about the Queen's belief in the power of dreams. You may believe the Queen gave up on her desire too soon or that she opened doors that shouldn't have been opened. Either way, those conversations seem to have affected you, or perhaps your friend confided in you because he saw something in you. Since childhood, your dreams have taken on a life of their own. Vivid and clear, they often seem to be telling you something important, although you can't always figure out what it is.

You seem to need more sleep than most people, and you often tinker with numenera items in an attempt to further connect with (or disconnect from) your dreams. If your skills are not a secret, some may seek you as a portent teller, while others may shun you or fear you.

You gain the following characteristics:

Dreamer: +2 to your Intellect Pool.

Contact: You remain close friends with the explorer who once worked for Queen Whenith Sarromere.

Skill: You are trained in all tasks involving glimmers and connecting with the datasphere.

Skill: You are trained in all tasks involving identifying or understanding the numenera.

Inability: Sometimes you have a hard time telling the real world from the dream world. The difficulty of all tasks involving discerning reality, telling truth from lie, or seeing through disguises is increased by one step.

Additional Equipment: You have a numenera device that you attach to your head while you sleep. You believe that it helps you to understand your dream visions (or, alternatively, that it helps to block them).

Initial Link to the Starting Adventure: From the following list of options, choose how you became involved in the first adventure.

1. You heard rumors that one of the PCs had an odd connection to her dreams, and you intend to check it out.

2. Multiple dreams seemed to lead you here.

3. One of the PCs heard about your skills and asked you to help guide them.

4. You're always seeking numenera devices to further your understanding, and the PCs' mission seems like a good opportunity to discover some.

PYTHARON

You grew up hearing the history of your kingdom—how the Pytharon Empire fell from great heights and then regained its former glory through determination, hard work, and smart weapons. Your heroes are the underdogs, the ones most likely to lose who pull off a win by the skin of their teeth and the edges of their blades. When the chips are down, when the tide turns against you, this is when you're at your strongest. You excel at being the underdog, changing the course of any situation from the bottom of the heap.

When things go smoothly, that's when you get bored and end up looking for trouble. It's as though you're not happy or functional unless you're fighting an uphill battle.

You likely wear an outfit that looks like nothing special to untrained eyes but is designed to offer protection and ease of movement. Your weapons might be the same—items that don't seem too intimidating, at least not until you're down in the dirt and start showing your true skills.

You gain the following characteristics:

Underdog: While you are impaired, you function as if you were hale. While you are debilitated, you function as if you were impaired. In other words, you don't suffer the effects of being impaired until you become debilitated, and you never suffer the effects of being debilitated. You still die if all your stat Pools are 0.

Skill: You're at your best when you're losing a fight and the odds are stacked against you. You are trained in all tasks involving recovery from disease, poison, or drugs.

Skill: You are trained in all Might defense tasks.

Inability: You aren't great at making the first move. The difficulty of any initiative actions (to determine who goes first in combat) is increased by one step.

Additional Equipment: You have an additional weapon, probably something small and hidden, that has seen you through many battles.

Initial Link to the Starting Adventure: From the following list of options, choose how you became involved in the first adventure.

1. The PCs are clearly unprepared for this mission, and you will help them get back on top.

2. You're utterly bored, and this mission seems like it offers a chance of adventure.

3. In a fit of boredom you picked a fight with the wrong person. Now they're coming after you, and you believe this group will be fun in combat.

Pytharon is a realm that typifies the passage of time, but in Ninth World terms. In other words, it is an old place with a lot of history, but only in respect to the other kingdoms of the Steadfast. Compared to some of the truly ancient aspects of the world, Pytharon—and all of Ninth World history—is not even a blink of an eye.

The Pytharon Empire, page 161

4. You helped one of the PCs in a recent combat, and he asked you to come along so the whole group can benefit from your skills.

MILAVIAN

Milave, page 163

Ancuan, page 166

Just like your home nation of Milave, you are fiercely independent. You probably don't want to lead, but you certainly don't want to follow. Working side by side with others is fine as long as you're given your autonomy and no one expects you to answer to them. Whether this desire to be self-sufficient stems from past experiences or is just a quirk of your personality, it is the driving force behind your choices.

You dress your own way, go your own way, and carve your own path. You would rather have someone make fun of you for being different than follow the most common path without questioning it. Sometimes you fight for your freedom so fiercely that you go in a direction you don't want to go, just to prove to others that you can.

You gain the following characteristics:

Independent: +2 to a stat Pool of your choice.

Skill: You are trained in one task of your choice.

Skill: You are trained in resisting mental effects.

Additional Equipment: You have a piece of paper rolled in a small metal tube. The paper stipulates that if you're ever captured and forced to live under someone else's rule, you want to be put to death.

Initial Link to the Starting Adventure: From the following list of options, choose how you became involved in the first adventure.

1. Someone told you not to get involved, so you became determined to join the party.

2. You instigated the whole thing and convinced the others to join you.

3. One of the PCs asked you to come along, and you surprised yourself by saying yes.

4. You need the money, and most of the PCs seemed like people who would let you do your own thing.

ANCUANI

Although your land is mostly fertile, diverse, and peaceful, these are not the things that speak to you. Instead, you're connected to the wilder side of Ancuan, the shores where pirates, murderers, barbarians, and thieves rule with wild abandon. You may not be a criminal, but you understand their ways, perhaps even better than they do. Whether you embrace your barbaric side or you try to be a soft, gentle soul, you just can't seem

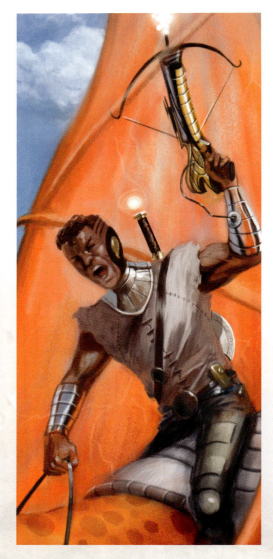

to move through the world with anything but savagery. Everything you do, you do it with a wild fierceness that makes others fear you.

You might dress to intimidate the hapless souls who cross you or to blend in with others who work the dangerous edges of the world. Your weapons are probably barbaric and brutal, and you know how to wield them better than most.

You gain the following characteristics:

Savage: +4 to your Might Pool.

Skill: You are trained in all noncombat tasks dealing with brute force, from breaking open doors to bending bars.

Skill: You speak the language of the savage. You are trained in all social interaction tasks that deal with criminals, barbarians, and brutes (including abhumans).

Inability: You are all power and no finesse. The difficulty of all tasks involving attention to detail, concentration, or focused movements is increased by one step.

Additional Equipment: You wear a saw-toothed claw on a string around your neck.

Initial Link to the Starting Adventure: From the following list of options, choose how you became involved in the first adventure.

1. You seek revenge on someone or something, and this mission is a means to an end.

2. You're trying to leave your barbaric ways behind by going on missions such as this one.

3. You believe that the PCs will die without your protection.

4. One of the PCs asked you to come along due to your ability to communicate with the savages of the world.

THE BEYOND

EPHREM

There is no place you feel more comfortable than high above the earth. Not flying—no, thank you—but climbing, swinging, or perching. Although you are most agile among the treetops, thanks to your time in

Ephremon, there is no structure so high that you won't at least attempt to reach its pinnacle. You prefer to fight from high above the ground—a vantage point in a nearby tree, perhaps, or a bit of hand-to-hand combat on a treacherous walkway.

You likely dress in the green, brown, and yellow camouflage of your homeland, and your clothes allow great freedom of moment. You might wear special gloves designed to help you scale even the sheerest of walls, and your equipment is well sealed and unobtrusive so that nothing will fall out or get in your way as you move.

You gain the following characteristics:

Acrobatic: +2 to your Speed Pool and +2 to your Might Pool.

Believer: You believe in the power of your god Falgreen to never let you fall. This faith is so strong that you can call upon it once per day to inspire you and give you +2 to your recovery roll.

Skill: You are trained in all tasks involving climbing, jumping, and balancing.

Inability: The earth is not your friend. The difficulty of all tasks involving geology and geography is increased by one step.

Additional Equipment: You carry a small statue of Falgreen to bring you luck and to keep you from the Last Great Fall.

Initial Link to the Starting Adventure: From the following list of options, choose how you became involved in the first adventure.

1. You heard rumors of some sort of giant structure, and you'd like to see it and, ideally, reach the pinnacle.

2. One of the other PCs convinced you to come so the group could benefit from your skills.

3. There is a reward involved, and you need the money.

4. One of the NPCs involved is a longtime friend, and you want to help out.

BAZIAN

Since you were little, automatons have been your best friends. In fact, until you were old enough to leave the Weal of Baz, you might

not have realized that you were human. Despite sharing a genetic code with the human race, you struggle to understand and connect with most of them.

You probably don't care at all about what you wear, and if you do care about style, you're likely to emulate the shined metal and synth of your autonomic friends. You might have

Ephremon, page 190

The Weal of Baz, page 198

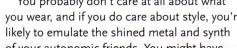

integrated bits and pieces of machines into your body in an effort to become less like an organic being and more like the machine that you know in your heart you should be. There's a good chance that your pack is more of a toolbelt, with various tools jangling from it, and that your weapon is one of a kind, made from various spare parts and bits of the numenera.

You gain the following characteristics:

Machine Mind: +2 to your Intellect Pool.

Austere: You are used to surviving without creature comforts. You can create a makeshift bed out of simple surroundings and scrape together food where others cannot. You give a sense of comfort to your companions, often accidentally. As a result, everyone in your group (except you, because these things don't seem to affect you much) gains +1 on all recovery rolls that take one hour or longer.

Matheunis, The Cold Desert, page 208

Connected: You understand the datasphere better than most (which still isn't very much), and once a day, you can tap into it and get the answer to a single question.

Skill: Understanding how automatons work and think is second nature to you. You are trained in creating, repairing, and communicating with automatons.

Inability: More often than not, people and their actions confuse and confound you. The difficulty of all tasks involving communication with humans, abhumans, and visitants is increased by one step.

Additional Equipment: You have an extra stash of spare parts and tools.

Initial Link to the Starting Adventure: From the following list of options, choose how you became involved in the first adventure.

1. You fixed an item for one of the PCs, and he asked you to come along.

2. There is a reward involved, and you need the money.

3. One of the automatons that lives in the area suggested that your skills would be useful on this adventure.

4. Someone talked to you about something and you apparently said yes, but you really have no idea what they were talking about or what you've gotten yourself into.

ICEBOUND

To most people, the Cold Desert means nothing but hardship and death, served up on an icy platter. But to you, a child of the icebound, the cold that kills many is nothing more than a passing irritation. In fact, freezing climes and places invigorate you and instill a sense of strength in you. Whether slipping across frozen lakes, stamping through deep snow, or surviving a whirling blizzard, you see the cold as a creature—one that you know and understand fully.

Your clothing is carefully designed to regulate your body temperature, even in the harshest weather, and you likely have created

or purchased multiple accessories or physical enhancements to further offset the effects of wind, ice, and snow.

You gain the following characteristics:

Gelid: +2 to your Might Pool.

Skill: You are trained in all noncombat tasks that involve snow or ice, including tracking, ice fishing, trekking, and geology.

Skill: To protect yourself from snow blindness, you have always taken good care of your eyes, using goggles, numenera devices, or mechanical enhancements. You are trained in all noncombat tasks involving vision, including perception, long-range sight, and seeing in dark or smoky areas.

Skill: In the middle of permafrost, a good campfire can be your best—and sometimes only—friend. You are trained in all noncombat tasks involving the use of fire, including creating, extinguishing, and controlling it.

Overheated: The sun is your foulest enemy. The difficulty of all tasks attempted in hot weather, dry climates, wastelands, or deserts is increased by one step.

Additional Equipment: You have a mutated drakka companion that alerts you to impending weather changes.

Initial Link to the Starting Adventure: From the following list of options, choose how you became involved in the first adventure.

1. One of the other PCs did a favor for you, and now you're repaying that obligation by helping her with the task at hand.

2. A colleague requested that you take part in the mission as a favor.

3. Someone mentioned your abilities to one of the PCs, who thought you'd be a perfect addition to the group.

4. You're afraid the PCs might fail if you don't assist them.

WASTELAND

You were raised in one of the Ninth World's many wastelands. Perhaps you hail from the barren, glassy stretch of the Jagged Wastes, or

maybe your home is one of the many pocket badlands that dot the Beyond. Harsh conditions, fierce predators, and a complete lack of civilization: these are the elements that make you feel most at home. You're ever alert, ready for anything, and few things take you by surprise.

For dress, you likely choose utility over style. Probably whatever you wear is hand-created from the skins, bones, and furs of your many slaughters, allowing you to blend into your surroundings while still showing off your conquests.

You gain the following characteristics:

Hardy: +2 to your Might Pool.

Solitary: Although you might enjoy the company of others, you're used to working alone. At least two members of your party must offer to assist you at the same time in order to decrease the difficulty of your task by one step.

Skill: Living off the land when there is barely anything to live off is just one of the many skills that has kept you alive. You are trained in noncombat tasks involving knowledge of area flora and fauna. This might include identifying and using plants, tracking prey, and finding potable water sources.

Skill: You're always on the alert and ready to take action. You're trained in all actions involving initiative (to determine who goes first in combat).

Additional Equipment: You have an oddity in the shape of a square rubber box that always has at least a spoonful of water in it, no matter how much you drink.

Initial Link to the Starting Adventure: From the following list of options, choose how you became involved in the first adventure.

1. One of the other PCs did a favor for you, and now you're repaying that obligation by helping her with the task at hand.

2. You overheard the other PCs discuss their mission and volunteered your services.

3. You're afraid that a horrible fate will befall the PCs if you don't assist them.

4. You're ready for a break from the harshness of the wastelands, and this seems like an easy job.

Wasteland characters often bear physical scars or other traits due to the environment in which they lived. On the other hand, it is the Ninth World, and thus scars can be artificially manufactured or made to permanently disappear, depending on one's desires.

Drakka, page 209
Dessanedi, the Jagged Wastes, page 187

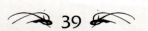

RACIAL OPTIONS

The assumption in Numenera is that all characters are human (although that word, *human*, can mean a lot of things in the Ninth World). However, there are exceptions. Racial characteristics are always expressed as descriptors, and this section presents four races—diruk, golthiar, mlox, and nalurus—that can replace more conventional descriptors.

Players can create nonhuman characters if the GM allows it. A nonhuman's race is his descriptor, but he can choose any character type and focus. For example, a player might choose a golthiar glaive who Murders or a mlox nano who Crafts Illusions. Because nonhuman characters gain more benefits from their racial type than they would from a conventional descriptor, each carries more disadvantages as well. Nonhuman characters also present roleplaying challenges, so it's recommended that new players do not create nonhuman PCs.

Visitants, page 120

RACIAL OPTIONS TABLE

Diruk	Mlox
Golthiar	Nalurus
Lattimor*	Varjellen*

* Racial options marked with asterisks appear in the Numenera corebook.

VISITANTS

The optional rules in the Numenera corebook include the visitants, which are different racial options for PCs. Visitants hail from...elsewhere. They are the descendants of travelers who came to Earth during a prior world, when interstellar—perhaps even intergalactic—travel was commonplace. Visitants now call the Ninth World home. They have dwelled on Earth for a thousand generations or more and have long forgotten any useful knowledge their ancestors may have had about science, technology, or the universe. Instead, they have adapted, biologically and culturally, to survive in their new home. They know no other life and no other place, but they remain keenly aware that they are at best transplants and at worst castaways.

This section offers a new type of visitant, the diruk.

DIRUK

In places far from the towns and other settlements sprinkled across the countryside, people tell tales of the living rocks. These creatures are known as the "wisdoms in the stone" to the nomads of the Dessanedi, and as the "voice of the gods" to the hermits and anchorites who pass their days in the Cold Desert of Matheunis. The names, while descriptive, erroneously assign a supernatural aspect to what are, in fact, a people who have chosen to live far from lands settled and controlled by humanity. Anyone seeing a diruk, as they call themselves, understands why so much mystery and wonder surrounds them. They look like beings made from rock, crystal, and metal.

No two diruks are alike. Each is a unique configuration of inorganic materials. Most have bodies made from some sort of stone

flecked with transparent crystals. Some look like raw ore, while others appear to be formed from clear crystal. Diruks can be quite small, the size of a rock a person can hold in one hand, or massive, standing two or three times the height of a human and looking more like a walking boulder. Most diruks are a bit taller than humans and weigh up to ten times a human's weight.

Diruks don't fill an ecological niche, which leads many people to speculate about where they came from. They don't breathe or consume organic materials, and they avoid water. Instead they absorb the same materials from which they are made, ingesting the stuff through a central orifice. Intense inner heat melts the materials and turns them into energy the diruks use to live and repair damage to their bodies from exposure or violence.

Diruks have no gender and find the concept utterly alien. They understand that organics reproduce through mating, but they consider the process strange and disturbing. When a diruk chooses to reproduce, it simply creates a nodule somewhere on its body, and when that nodule attains sufficient size and personality, it snaps off to find its own way in the world.

Diruks recognize differences among themselves by the materials making up their bodies. Those made of finer substances hold higher places in their social circles, while those of base materials tend to be at the bottom. Thus, diruk leaders have crystalline bodies, and the "common" people may be sandstone, granite, or lead.

In general, diruks distrust humans because at various points, humanity has exploited them for labor or hunted them for the precious materials their bodies contain. As a result, diruks are reluctant to deal with humans and may become aggressive if trespassers come onto their lands.

Most humans consider diruks cold, impassive, and much like the rocks they resemble. Part of the problem stems from the diruks' inability to match human body language or expressions. They may not be expressive in the ways that humans are, but they supplement their speech by venting smoke from fissures in their bodies or changing the colors of the crystals embedded in their stony hides. When a diruk's crystals shine green, it is pleased and happy. When they show red, it is angry to the point that it might use violence to solve its troubles. Blue

suggests sadness, pink implies affection, yellow curiosity, and other colors signify moods and emotions beyond human capacity to understand.

Diruks sometimes leave their homelands to start new colonies. They wander the world for years or decades searching for the ideal place to make their home and produce offspring. It is during these rovings that diruks are likely to come into contact with and maybe live alongside humans.

Diruk Characteristics

All diruk characters in Numenera have the following characteristics:

Stone Body: +3 to Armor. However, you gain no benefit from wearing armor.

Mighty: Your Might Edge increases by 2.

Skill: You are trained in carrying and smashing things.

Inability: The difficulty of all Speed tasks increases by one step.

Inability: You are not expressive, and others have a hard time understanding you. The difficulty of tasks involving interacting with others in a pleasant manner is increased by one step.

Inability: You are slow to react. The difficulty of initiative tasks (to see who goes first in combat) increases by one step.

Inability: You are slow. The difficulty of running tasks increases by one step.

Inability: You sink like a stone in water. The difficulty of swimming tasks increases by one step.

NONHUMAN RACES

It's possible for Numenera players to create characters that would normally be considered "creatures" of the world. These are not visitants (that's a fairly specific group of creatures) but other nonhuman intelligent beings. Many creatures in the Ninth World carry enough humanity that they can become player characters. Golthiars, mloxan, and naluruses are just a few options, although others exist.

GOLTHIAR

Golthiars are humanoid creatures, about 6.5 feet (2 m) tall, composed of barklike skin and woody muscle. A golthiar's single eye rests in the middle of a bulbous, petalled head, all of which resides atop a long, stalklike neck.

Born fully formed out of underground seed

Like other visitants, diruks can be found anywhere. However, there is a large gathering of them along the southern rim of the Clock of Kala, and another in the western portion of the Cold Desert.

Golthiars, mloxan, and naluruses are taken from The Ninth World Bestiary, *but that book is not required to use them as character options.*

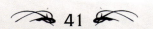

pods, golthiars can subsist on little more than sun and drit. However, to gather the necessary nutrients, they must bury themselves deep in a drit patch every few days.

Most golthiars live and act in groups of four or more, assisting each other with combat and defense. They typically coordinate their attacks through the use of beamed color that is invisible to most humans. As a general rule, golthiars communicate via pulsing beams of light, a language that is notoriously difficult to decipher.

Although golthiars as a race are diverse in both appearance and personality, there is one thing that most share: a purpose in life. For a golthiar, nothing is more important than the job at hand, whether that means guarding something, attacking something, or scouting something. Those without jobs or orders to follow often begin to wither within a few months. Death is likely to follow.

Most golthiars move in groups of four or more. Thus, players who choose to play a golthiar should have a backstory on why their character has gone rogue.

Occasionally, a golthiar goes rogue, breaking off from its companions at an early age and attempting to go it alone. Most find this difficult at best, but the smartest and most adaptable find a place among human civilization, usually by learning to communicate and making themselves indispensable as guards, scouts, or fighters.

Golthiar Characteristics

All golthiar characters in Numenera have the following characteristics:

Fierce Defender: +1 to Armor.

Solar: Once per day, if the sun is shining, you may stand in direct sunlight as an action to restore 1 point to each of your stat Pools without a roll.

Skill: You are trained in all tasks involving botany or geology.

Skill: You are trained in all tasks that involve learning, decoding, or understanding languages.

Skill: As a naturally communal creature, you connect deeply to those around you. You are trained in all skills involving honest social interaction.

Inability: You don't react well to surprises. The difficulty of all tasks involving the use of initiative is increased by one step.

Blind: You are particularly sensitive to unexpected light. A flash of bright light from any source increases the difficulty of your next action by one step.

Deficient: Once every three days, you must take one hour to bury yourself in drit to receive the necessary nutrients from the soil. Doing so has no positive effect, but if you fail to do so, you lose 5 points from your Might Pool that day and each subsequent day until you take this action.

Aimless: If, for some reason, you have no purpose set before you—be it guarding something, scouting an area, or fighting for a higher goal—you begin to feel morose and lethargic. The difficulty of any task that doesn't move you toward finding a new purpose is increased by one step.

MLOX

Based on outward appearances, a mlox is nearly impossible to distinguish from a human, except for one outstanding physical feature: a mlox can iris open a portion of his forehead, revealing a mechanical glowing "third eye." This eye is actually the leading edge of a mechanical brain that fills a mlox's entire brain cavity.

With their machine minds and biological bodies, mloxan are both hardier than humans and more fragile, in entirely different ways. Their mechanical brains make them quick to perceive and adapt to their surroundings, but only when their third eye is open. With this extra view on the world, mloxan can connect more directly to their surroundings, gaining unique abilities.

As a race, mloxan are secretive, often hiding their real form behind the guise of humanity. They are unlikely to reveal their odd anatomy except when under duress or, rarely, in the company of people they truly and deeply trust.

When passing as human, their mloxan senses are dulled and their reactions slightly slower than typical. However, they gain different talents in human guise, such as an exceptional ability to blend in with the human race. They are good with languages, not just learning whatever languages are in their area, but quickly picking up on dialects, slang, and accents. Additionally, they are excellent emulators and quick learners, copying the common style of dress and speech in an area and even changing their body language to best suit the person they're communicating with. They are also joiners; it's not unusual to find a handful of mloxan hiding deep inside organizations, religious entities, town councils, or other groups.

Mloxan typically take on traditional physical elements of humans, including gender, but they can't interbreed with humans or visitants. In fact, it's unknown how mloxan reproduce. Perhaps they can't, or perhaps this is one of the many secrets that they keep to themselves.

Most mloxan avoid conflict whenever they can. If they must fight, they do so with simple human weapons, using no unusual skills, often taking a defensive pose. Only with their third eye open do they show themselves to be skilled combatants, with quick reflexes and strong defenses.

Mlox Characteristics

Transitioning between your human guise and your mloxan form (essentially, irising your third eye open) is an action. You can change forms as many times as you like, with each new transition requiring an action.

All mlox characters in Numenera have the following characteristics:

Fragile: The connection between your mechanical brain and your biological body isn't a perfect one, and it leaves you vulnerable to injury and illness. At first tier, you have 4 points, not 6, to divide among your stat Pools.

When in mloxan form:

Reflexive: +2 to your Speed Pool.

Protected: When your third eye is open, you project a force screen around yourself, gaining 1 point of Armor. Enabler.

Unaffected: While in mloxan form, you may carry one extra cypher above your normal allowance. Upon returning to your human guise, your cypher allowance returns to normal.

Skill: You are trained in Speed defense tasks.

Skill: You are trained in visual and auditory perception.

Skill: You are trained in all noncombat tasks pertaining to Speed and reflexes.

Inability: The difficulty of all tasks involving deception, sneaking, and camouflage is increased by one step.

Inability: The difficulty of all tasks involving charm, persuasion, and etiquette is increased by one step.

Inability: The difficulty of all tasks requiring knowledge, memory, or lore is increased by one step.

Additional Equipment: You have one extra cypher above your normal allowance (to be chosen by the GM).

When in human guise:

Skill: You are trained in deception, sneaking, and camouflage.

Skill: You are trained in all tasks involving charm, persuasion, and etiquette.

Skill: You are trained in all tasks requiring knowledge, memory, or lore.

Inability: Without your third eye open, it's harder for you to discern your surroundings and react efficiently. The difficulty of all noncombat tasks involving speed and perception is increased by one step.

NALURUS

Most naluruses would argue that they are strictly human, but they know better—as does anyone who catches so much as a glimpse of their face. It is true that naluruses could

Despite—or perhaps because of—their internal mechanized brains, mloxan are particularly distrustful of all mechanical creatures and attempt to stay far away from them.

Mloxan may have secret names that are known only to themselves, but the names they offer to others are typically very common and very human (and have probably changed over time).

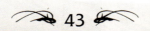

once stake a claim to humanity, but for most of them, that is long past. Now, a nalurus is a truly dangerous creature, crippled by the terrible disease that courses through its body.

A nalurus looks like a stooped and fragile human in all ways except for its head, which is covered with a unique pattern of spirals, geometric shapes, and disquieting lines, a remnant of the disease that nearly killed him. This lasting symbol of the disease is also contagious, for a nalurus transmits its infection by sight.

If a human, visitant, or abhuman sees a nalurus without its hood, the awful pattern of its face imprints on the viewer's mind, setting off a rapid and painful chain reaction. Less than a minute after the victim catches a glimpse of the patterns, his brain liquefies and runs out his eyes, nose, mouth, and ears as pinkish fluid.

A sane nalurus in the company of humans

always wears a hood or a mask over its face to protect them from infection.

Nalurus Characteristics

All nalurus characters in Numenera have the following characteristics:

Survivor: +2 to your Might Pool.

Self-Healing: The disease you carry doesn't affect you the way that it does others. If you look at your own face in a highly reflective surface while healing, your disease gives you +1 to all recovery rolls.

Liability: Those fighting or taking other actions near you must take extra care not to catch a glimpse of your face. Anyone attempting a task within immediate range finds that the difficulty of that task is increased by one step.

Skill: You are trained in all stealth tasks.

Skill: You are trained in all noncombat tasks that involve healing, poison, or disease.

Skill: You are trained in camouflage, deception, and intimidation.

Inability: You are often in pain and worried about accidentally showing your face, and this makes you gruff and discourteous. The difficulty of all tasks relating to persuasion or charm is increased by one step.

Inability: With your head down, your vision is sometimes blocked by your mask or the edges of your hood. The difficulty of all tasks relating to perception is increased by one step.

Additional Equipment: You have a face mask or hood. You also carry a unique walking staff to assist you with your stooped appearance. It can also be used as a medium weapon.

MUTANTS

Some characters have been affected by mutation. Mutants are not visitants. They are humans who have changed over time, either through natural forces of evolution or through an unnatural manipulation—intentional or not—of an individual or his ancestors. Unnatural manipulation could mean exposure to mutagens, the result of genetic engineering, or the result of genetic engineering gone wrong.

In the Ninth World, mutants sometimes band together. Those with hideous deformities face discrimination and derision. Some are outcasts, and others are revered, flaunting their mutations as a sign of superiority, power, and influence. Their mutations are seen as a blessing, not a curse. Some people believe them to be divine.

There are five categories of mutations. Two of them—beneficial mutations and powerful mutations—bring about changes that are neither physically obvious nor extraordinary. Powerful mutations are more potent than beneficial ones. Harmful mutations are physical changes that are usually grotesque and somewhat debilitating. The fourth category, distinctive mutations, also provides significant abilities, but they mark the character as an obvious mutant. Last, cosmetic mutations bring no special capabilities at all and are merely cosmetic (although sometimes dramatically so).

In theory, there is a sixth category that might be called crippling mutations, but characters never have this kind of mutation. Mutants with crippling mutations might be born without limbs, with barely functional lungs, without most of their brain, and so on. Such mutations prevent a character from being viable.

If you want to play a mutant, you have special abilities, but they come at a cost. In lieu of a descriptor—or rather, by choosing *mutant* as your descriptor—you gain two beneficial mutations. If you opt to take a harmful mutation as well, you can have three beneficial mutations, or one powerful mutation, or one distinctive mutation. You can also have from zero to four distinctive mutations, which is completely up to you. Mutations are always rolled randomly, although the player and GM can work together to ensure that the resulting character is one that the player wants to play.

Unlike abilities gained from most other sources, mutations that affect the difficulty of tasks are assets, not skills. That means any step changes from a mutation are in addition to any step changes you might have from a skill.

BENEFICIAL MUTATIONS

The following mutations do not require any visible changes or distinctions in the character. In other words, people who have these mutations are not obviously recognized as mutants. Using beneficial mutations never costs stat Pool points and never requires an action to "activate."

01–50 Corebook: Use the table on page 124 of the Numenera corebook.

51–54 Boneless: You have cartilage instead of bones. You can wriggle through tight spaces and slip free from bonds. You have an asset on any task that involves contortions or escaping.

55–60 Empathy: You feel other people's moods and emotions. You have an asset on any task to determine another creature's motives or emotional state, or to see through lies and other deceptions.

61–65 Improved jumping: You have an asset on any task involving jumping.

66–69 Remarkable poise: You have near-perfect balance. You have an asset on any task that involves balancing.

70–74 Machine interface: You have an asset on any task involving understanding, operating, or repairing a numenera device.

75–79 Eagle eyes: You have an asset on any visual perception task.

80–83 Polyglot: When you hear a language spoken for at least one minute, you can communicate in that language as a native speaker for 28 hours.

84–87 Precognition: You catch glimpses of the future. You have an asset on all initiative tasks.

88–90 Eat anything: You can eat whatever you can fit inside your mouth and be nourished by it.

91–94 Echolocation: You can "see" sound. You can see invisible creatures and objects within short range.

95–97 Sense mutation: You are aware of the presence of any mutants within short range, even if those mutants are hidden from you.

98–99 Kinetic absorption: You can absorb harmful energy and redirect it at others. When you take damage as a result of failing a Speed defense roll, you have an asset on the next attack roll you make before the end of your next turn. If your attack fails or you don't attack during your next turn, you take 3 additional points of damage.

00 Minor spacewarp: By very briefly foreshortening distance, you increase the range of any attack you make by one step. Immediate-range attacks become short range, short-range attacks become long range, and long-range attacks have a range of 200 feet (61 m).

HARMFUL MUTATIONS

Unless noted otherwise, the following mutations are visible, obvious, and grotesque. They offer no benefits, only drawbacks.

01–70 Corebook: Use the table on page 124 of the Numenera corebook.

71–72 Accidental combustion: Once per day or so, a flammable object that you touch or that is next to you ignites in flame.

Since many mutations are not at all physical or even visible, there may be many more mutants in the Ninth World than most people know.

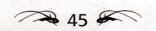

73–74 Accidental psychokinesis: Once per day or so, an object that you touch or that is next to you moves violently, often breaking the object, but sometimes harming you or someone in immediate range (2 points of damage).

75–77 Debilitating telepathy: You are sometimes (usually once a day) afflicted by random bouts of cacophonous telepathy when thinking beings are within immediate range. You never gain valuable information, but for ten minutes, the overwhelming din in your head increases the difficulty of all tasks by one step.

78–80 Horrific precognition: You are sometimes (usually once a day) afflicted by random visions of the future where you or others within immediate range are hurt, killed, or otherwise harmed. You never gain valuable information, but for one minute, the shock increases the difficulty of all tasks by one step.

81–82 Hidden twin: A parasitic consciousness lives inside you. It grumbles and mutters to you all the time, causing you to be distracted and confused by the constant noise that only you can hear. The difficulty of all initiative and perception tasks is increased by one step.

83–87 Light blindness: You cannot see in areas of light and are blinded in such areas. However, you can see normally in dim light or darker conditions.

88–90 Membrane: You don't have skin. Instead, your epidermis is a milky, gelatinous membrane. Because it dries and cracks, you must keep it damp. Each hour you go without immersing yourself in water for at least one minute, you take 1 point of damage (ambient).

91–92 No mouth: You have no mouth and cannot talk. You consume sustenance in some other way that you and your GM agree to.

93–97 Horribly ugly: You are hideously deformed. The difficulty of all pleasant social interaction tasks is increased by one step.

98–99 Weak bones: Your Might Pool is decreased by 3 points.

00 Extraneous tendril: A nonprehensile tendril hangs uselessly from your body, always getting in the way. The difficulty of all movement actions is increased by one step.

POWERFUL MUTATIONS

The following mutations do not require any visible changes in the character until used. People who have these mutations are not obviously recognized as mutants if they don't use their powers. Using some of these mutations costs stat Pool points. Some are actions.

01–50 Corebook: Use the table on page 125 of the Numenera corebook.

51 Absorb mutation (4 Might points): You touch a creature and gain one of its mutations. Against an unwilling creature, you must succeed on a Might attack roll. Determine randomly which mutation you gain if the creature has more than one. You have the mutation for 1d20 minutes, after which time it fades away. Action.

52 Awaken beneficial mutation (3 Intellect points): You choose a creature within immediate range and cause it to gain a randomly determined beneficial mutation for

ten minutes. Against an unwilling creature, you must succeed on an Intellect attack roll. Action.

53 Awaken cosmetic mutation (1 Intellect point): You choose a creature within immediate range and cause it to gain a randomly determined cosmetic mutation for ten minutes. Against an unwilling creature, you must succeed on an Intellect attack roll. Action.

54 Awaken distinctive mutation (6 Intellect points): You choose a creature within immediate range and cause it to gain a randomly determined distinctive mutation for ten minutes. Against an unwilling creature, you must succeed on an Intellect attack roll. Action.

55 Awaken harmful mutation (7 Intellect points): You choose a creature within immediate range and cause it to gain a randomly determined harmful mutation for ten minutes. Against an unwilling creature, you must succeed on an Intellect attack roll. Action.

56 Awaken powerful mutation (10 Intellect points): You choose a creature within immediate range and cause it to gain a randomly determined powerful mutation for ten minutes. Against an unwilling creature, you must succeed on an Intellect attack roll. Action.

57–58 Light burst (3 Intellect points): You create a burst of light through your skin that potentially blinds all creatures within immediate range for 1d6 + 1 rounds. You are immune to the effect. Action.

59–60 Light beam (2 Intellect points): You emit a ray of harmful energy that inflicts 4 points of damage to a single target within long range. Action.

61–62 Deafening scream (4 Might points): You scream, stunning all creatures within immediate range for one round (during which time they cannot take actions on their turn), and deafening all creatures within immediate range for 1d6 + 1 rounds. You are immune to the effect. Action.

63–64 Poisonous breath (3 Might points): You exhale poisonous vapors that inflict 3 points of damage to all creatures within immediate range for one round. You are immune to the vapors. Action.

65 Astral projection (4 Intellect points): You visualize a place within long range and cast your mind to that place, creating an invisible sensor that you can move a short distance

each round for ten minutes or until you choose to end this ability. While using the projection, you see through your sensor instead of your eyes using your normal visual abilities. You may perceive the area around your body using your other senses as normal.

66–67 Freezing touch (2 Intellect points): Your touch inflicts 4 points of damage due to the extremely low temperatures of the air around you. Action.

68–69 Melting touch (2 Intellect points): Your touch inflicts 4 points of damage due to the heat you generate. Action.

70 Mimic action (3 Intellect points): If you observe an action that you could attempt, you can attempt it on the following round as if you possessed the skill you observed. For example, if you watch someone specialized in climbing climb a wall, you can attempt to climb as though specialized. You can't attempt something that you can't do (for example, you cannot use a mutant power or esotery that you don't possess). Action to observe, action to attempt.

71–72 Access information (2 Intellect points): You can mentally tap into the datasphere and gain an asset on any topic or area of knowledge. Action.

73 Rotting touch (2 Might points): Organic material that you touch (including living flesh) disintegrates. This inflicts 4 points of damage. Action.

74 Corrosive touch (2 Might points): Inorganic material that you touch disintegrates. This inflicts 4 points of damage. Action.

75 Possession (5+ Intellect points): You control the actions of another creature that

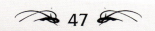

you touch. This effect lasts for ten minutes, during which time you can take no actions with your normal body. The target must be level 2 or lower. Once you have established control, you sense what the target senses as if you were that creature. You can allow it to act freely or override its control on a case-by-case basis. Instead of applying Effort to decrease the difficulty, you can apply Effort to increase the maximum level of the target. Thus, to possess a level 5 target (three levels above the normal limit), you must apply three levels of Effort. When the possession ends, the creature doesn't remember being controlled or anything it did while under your command. Action to initiate.

76 Alter memories (3 Intellect points): You alter a specific memory in the mind of a creature you touch. You must have some foreknowledge that the creature has the memory you wish to alter. You can make the creature forget the real memory and replace it with anything you like. Obviously, something similar or at least realistic will cause less suspicion later. Action.

77 Teeth spew (3 Might points): You vomit a spray of bile and broken teeth that affects up to three targets within immediate range if they are all next to each other. Each target suffers 3 points of damage. You rapidly regrow the teeth you lose in this act. Action.

78 Acidic spew (3 Might points): You vomit a spray of acidic goo that affects up to three targets within immediate range if they are all next to each other. Each target suffers 3 points of damage. Action.

79–80 Rapid recovery: Your ten-minute recovery roll takes one action instead, so that your first two recovery rolls take one action, the third takes one hour, and the fourth takes ten hours. Enabler.

81–82 Ignore pain: You ignore the impaired condition and treat the debilitated condition as impaired. Enabler.

83 Burst of speed (2 Speed points): Your speed doubles for one round. Enabler.

84 Dampen light (2 Intellect points): You reduce light levels within short range. Light in the area becomes dim light, dim light becomes very dim light, and very dim light becomes darkness. The area of reduced light moves with you until the effect ends. The effect lasts for ten minutes or until you choose to end it using an action. Action to initiate.

85 Excrete corrosive (3 Might points): You excrete a syrupy corrosive material from your hand. If you wipe it off on a metal surface, the goo corrodes the metal, dealing 4 points of damage. Otherwise, the excretion dries after one minute and flakes away. Action.

86 Fuse (5 Might points): You can merge your body with that of a willing creature within immediate range. You flow into that creature's body and can remain there for up to one hour. Until this effect ends, you cannot use actions, but you perceive what the creature perceives and you can communicate with that creature. Action.

87 Invisibility (5 Intellect points): You fade from view and have no appearance for one minute. While invisible, you are specialized in stealth and Speed defense tasks. This effect ends if you do something to reveal your presence or position—attacking, performing an esotery, using an ability, moving a large object, and so on. If this occurs, you can regain the remaining invisibility effect by taking an action to focus on hiding your position. Action to initiate or reinitiate.

88 Immortal: You are in the prime of your life. You do not age and are immune to anything that would age you. Enabler.

89 Merge (6 Might points): You merge your body with an object that is your size or larger that you can touch. You disappear into the object and can remain there for as long as you like. While inside the object, you are insensate regarding what happens outside of the object, but you know how much time has passed. If the object you are merged with is destroyed, you are destroyed with it. The only action you can take while in the object is to move out of it. Action to initiate.

90–91 Modify mass (3 Might points): You can increase your weight by up to 100% or decrease it by as much as 50% of your normal weight. The change in weight lasts for one hour. Action to initiate.

92 Petrify (5 Might points): You touch a creature and slowly turn it to a dry, hard, stonelike substance. On a success, the creature cannot move during its next turn

Eric Lofgren

and has +2 to Armor. If you touch the same creature three times in a row, the creature turns into a statue. Action.

93–94 Projection (3 Intellect points): You create a hologram of yourself in any spot you choose within short range. The illusion lasts for one minute or until anything touches it. It looks and sounds real, and it mimics your movements perfectly. Action to initiate.

95 Invisible extra arm: You have one invisible extra arm. It can hold objects, wield weapons, hold a shield, pick pockets, and so on. This mutation does not increase the number of actions you can take in a round or the number of attacks you can attempt. Enabler.

96 Resonance field (3 Intellect points): You focus your mind to augment numenera nearby. Characters within immediate range have an asset on any roll made to use numenera. The effect lasts for one minute. Action to initiate.

97 Vampire (2 Might points): You touch another creature and draw its physical energies to sustain your own. On a success, the creature takes 2 points of damage and you recover 1 point of damage. Action to initiate.

98–99 X-ray vision (5 Might points): You focus your vision to peer through a solid object. You see as if you were in a lighted area. Your vision can pierce up to 3 feet (0.9 m) of organic material, 1 foot (0.3 m) of stone, or 1 inch (2.5 cm) of metal. Your vision lasts for one minute. Action to initiate.

00 Invisible wings: You have invisible wings on your back that allow you to glide, carried by the wind. They are not powerful enough to carry you aloft like a bird's wings. Enabler.

DISTINCTIVE MUTATIONS

The following mutations typically involve dramatic physical changes to the character's appearance. People who have these mutations are almost always recognized as mutants. Using some of these mutations costs stat Pool points. Some are actions.

01–60 Corebook: Use the table on page 126 of the Numenera corebook.

61–62 Bone claws: You have bony spikes protruding from your hands or the backs of your arms. Your unarmed attacks deal 1 additional point of damage. Enabler.

63–64 Spurs: You have large, bony spurs on your elbows and knees that you can use as light weapons that inflict 1 additional point of damage. Enabler.

65–66 Detachable limb (3 Might points): You can detach an arm or leg from your body. You control this limb as if it were still attached, though only if it remains within long range. If you are separated by a distance greater than long range, the limb stops moving. You can reattach the limb at any time by picking it up and sticking it to the stump. Action to initiate.

67–68 Removable eye (2 Might points): You can pull out one of your eyes and still see through it as long as it's within long range. You must return the eye to its socket within an hour or you lose it. Action to initiate.

69–70 Extra eye(s) on stalk(s): You have one to three additional eyes on stalks. You can peek around corners without exposing yourself to danger. This is an asset in initiative and all perception tasks. Also roll on the beneficial mutations table. Enabler.

Eric Lofgren

71–72 Tail: You have a long tail that serves as an asset for balancing, climbing, and running tasks.

73–74 Enormous ears: Your enormous ears are especially sensitive. You have an asset on all perception tasks that involving listening. Enabler.

75–76 Modify limb (1 Might point): You cause a limb of your choice to grow up to twice its normal size or shrink to half its normal size. If you increase the size, you have an asset for any Might roll that involves using that limb, though not for attacks. The change in size lasts for one hour. Also roll on the beneficial mutations table. Action to initiate.

77–78 Mouths in your hands: You have a mouth in the palm of each hand. Neither of these mouths can speak, but they can eat and bite. Your unarmed attacks deal 1 additional point of damage. Enabler.

79–80 Prehensile tongue: Your tongue is flexible and 3 feet (0.9 m) long. You can use it to grasp objects, and you have an asset for all tasks involving grappling and wrestling. Also roll on the beneficial mutations table. Enabler.

81–82 Rampant evolution: Each day, roll on the cosmetic mutations table (page 128 of the Numenera corebook) and gain the result. The mutation remains until you use this mutation again. Also roll on the beneficial mutations table. Enabler.

83–84 Organic steel flesh: Your flesh is reminiscent of flexible metal. You have +3 to Armor, but you cannot wear other mundane armor as it is too encumbering. Enabler.

85–86 Amorphous arm (1 Might point): You can make one of your arms into amorphous goo that you control for one minute. It retains its normal strength but can ooze through cracks, can stretch up to three times its length, and is an asset if you try to suffocate a foe. Action to initiate.

87–88 Amorphous body (3 Might points): You can transform into amorphous goo for one minute. You retain your normal strength but move at half speed. You can ooze through cracks, can stretch up to three times your length, and have 2 additional points of Armor that apply only to piercing and slashing attacks. You gain an asset for climbing and an inability in jumping or running. Action to initiate.

89–90 Pseudopods: You have one or two pseudopods that can be used for rough grasping or half-speed locomotion. They can stretch as long as your normal arms. Enabler.

91–92 Tendrils on back: Two to four prehensile tendrils, each 6 feet (1.8 m) long, sprout from your back. They are not strong or dextrous enough to wield weapons, but they can manipulate light objects. Enabler.

93–94 Tentacles on face: Four to six tendrils, each 12 to 24 inches (30 to 61 cm) long, surround your mouth. They can grasp and carry anything that your hand could. Also roll on the beneficial mutations table. Enabler.

95–96 Gliding membrane: You have fleshy membranes between your arms and torso that allow you to glide, carried by the wind. They are not powerful enough to carry you aloft like a bird's wings. Enabler.

97–98 Huge claws: Your hands are medium weapons, and you have an asset when using them to attack. It's very difficult for you to perform delicate or precise tasks involving manual dexterity, and the difficulty of such tasks is increased by one step.

99–00 Uni-horn: You have a long horn on your forehead or the top of your head. You can use this as a medium weapon.

FOCI

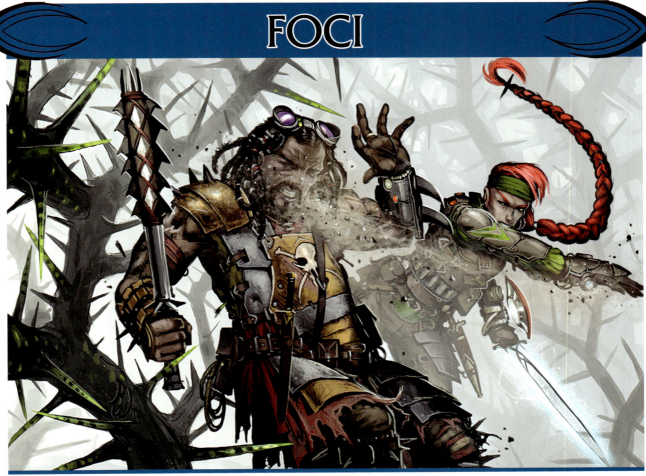

More than descriptor or type, focus is what makes your character unique. No two PCs in a group should have the same focus. Your focus gives you benefits when you create your character and each time you ascend to the next tier. It's the verb of the sentence "I am an *adjective noun* who *verbs*." The foci presented here supplement those found in the Numenera corebook. Some of them are much more specific or specialized, and others are just plain weird. In any case, they will be useful to many characters and of particular use in certain campaigns. With these new foci, it should be easier than ever to ensure that your character is unique, different from all the others in the group.

When you choose a character focus, you get a special connection to one or more of your fellow PCs, a first-tier ability, and perhaps additional starting equipment. A few foci offer slight alterations of esoteries or tricks for nanos and jacks. Each focus also offers suggestions to the GM and the player for possible effects or consequences of really good or really bad die rolls.

As you progress to a new tier, your focus grants you more abilities. Each tier's benefit is usually labeled *Action* or *Enabler*. If an ability is labeled Action, you must take an action to use it. If an ability is labeled Enabler, it makes other actions better or gives some other benefit, but it's not an action. An ability that allows you to blast foes with lasers is an action. An ability that grants you additional damage when you make attacks is an enabler. You can use an enabler in the same turn as you perform another action.

Each tier's benefits are independent of and cumulative with benefits from other tiers (unless indicated otherwise). So if your first-tier ability grants you +1 to Armor and your fourth-tier ability also grants you +1 to Armor, when you reach fourth tier, you have a total of +2 to Armor.

BATTLES AUTOMATONS

Life is for the living—the biological. Automatons, animate machines, thinking machines, and anything similar are abominations. You excel at battling these anathemas, cleansing the world of their contaminating presence.

FOCI TABLE

Battles Automatons	Fights With Panache*	Never Says Die
Bears a Halo of Fire*	Focuses Mind Over Matter*	Performs Feats of Strength
Carries a Quiver*	Focuses Two Personalities	Possesses a Shard of the Sun
Commands Mental Powers*	Fuses Flesh and Steel*	Rages*
Consorts With the Dead	Fuses Mind and Machine	Reforges Completely
Constantly Evolves	Howls at the Moon*	Rides the Lightning*
Controls Beasts*	Hunts Abhumans	Sees Beyond
Controls Gravity*	Hunts Mutants	Separates Mind From Body
Crafts Illusions*	Hunts With Great Skill*	Siphons Power
Crafts Unique Objects*	Leads*	Stands Like a Bastion
Defends the Weak	Lives in the Wilderness*	Talks to Machines*
Employs Magnetism*	Masters Defense*	Throws With Deadly Accuracy
Entertains*	Masters Insects	Travels Through Time
Exists in Two Places at Once	Masters Weaponry*	Wears a Sheen of Ice*
Exists Partially Out of Phase•	Metes Out Justice	Wields Power With Precision*
Explores Dark Places•	Moves Like a Cat	Wields Two Weapons at Once*
Explores Deep Waters	Murders*	Works Miracles*
Fights Dirty	Needs No Weapon	Works the Back Alleys*

* Foci marked with asterisks appear in the Numenera corebook.

Battles Automatons

GM Intrusions: *Not all automatons should be destroyed. Some might explode when defeated. Eventually, organized thinking machines will seek out and try to kill someone who seeks to destroy them.*

Maybe your desire to battle automatons comes from religious zealotry. Maybe it's steeped in revenge for some past crime committed by a machine. Maybe you don't know why you're driven to destroy animate machines. Maybe you're just good at it.

You probably bear the trophies of former "kills" on you, wearing bits of numenera on your belt or around your neck. You also likely use heavy weaponry, ideal for penetrating armor. Glaives are most often automaton fighters, particularly those who are quick and nimble, able to leap in and cut a few vital wires here, or slice through a component panel there.

Connection: Choose one of the following.

1. Pick one other PC. You suspect that this character is put off by your hatred of animate machines. You can choose whether or not she knows of your suspicions.

2. Pick one other PC. You know that this character has suffered at the hands of automatons in the past, and perhaps you can convince him to help you in your calling. Regardless, you feel protective of him.

3. Pick one other PC. This character does not appear to share your feelings about automatons. In fact, you believe that she might secretly have machine parts herself.

4. Pick one other PC. This character comes from the same place you do, and you knew each other as children.

Additional Equipment: You have bits and pieces that you tore from the husks of automatons you have destroyed in the past.

Anti-Machine Esoteries: If you perform esoteries, those that inflict damage inflict 1 additional point of damage to automatons and similar beings, and 1 less point of damage to biological, living targets. If you have esoteries that normally would not work against automatons, they will function against your enemy.

Minor Effect Suggestions: Your foe experiences an error for one round, during which time the difficulty of all tasks it performs is modified by one step to its detriment.

Major Effect Suggestions: Your foe experiences a major error and loses its next turn.

Tier 1: Machine Vulnerabilities. You inflict 3 additional points of damage against automatons and animate machines of all kinds. Enabler.

Numenera Knowledge. You are trained in the numenera. Enabler.

Tier 2: Defense Against Automatons. You have studied your enemy and can anticipate the actions that an automaton or machine is likely to take in a fight. The difficulty of all defense tasks against such foes is decreased by one

step. Enabler.

Machine Hunting. The difficulty of tracking, spotting, or otherwise finding automatons and animate machines is decreased by one step. You are also trained in all stealth tasks. Enabler.

Tier 3: Disable Mechanisms (3 Speed points). With a keen eye and quick moves, you disrupt some of an automaton's functions and inflict upon it one of the following maladies:
• The difficulty of all tasks is increased by one step for one minute.
• The speed of the automaton is halved.
• The automaton can take no action for one round.
• The automaton deals 2 fewer points of damage (minimum 1 point) for one minute.

You must touch the automaton to disrupt it (if you are making an attack, it inflicts no normal damage). Action.

Tier 4: Machine Fighter. You are trained in all attacks against automatons or similar animate machines. Enabler.

Pierce Metal Hides. You ignore 2 points of Armor on an automaton.

Tier 5: Drain Power (5 Speed points).

You affect the main power source of the automaton, inflicting upon it all four conditions listed for Disable Mechanisms at once. You must touch the automaton to do this (if you are making an attack, it inflicts no normal damage). Action.

Tier 6: Blind Machine (6 Speed points). You deactivate the sensory apparatus of the automaton, making it effectively blind. You must either touch the target or strike it with a ranged attack (inflicting no normal damage). Action.

CONSORTS WITH THE DEAD

Through the study of sciences to which most people give a wide berth, you have mastered the ability to speak with and reanimate the dead. The numenera holds no moral or ethical distinctions between different abilities or types of knowledge, but Ninth World society does, and necromancy is shunned as a taboo. Nothing that you do proves the existence of an afterlife—your abilities deal with retrieving information from brain cells and reactivating dead tissues. Still, perhaps delving even deeper into your studies can reveal knowledge of what happens after death and whether it's possible to truly restore the dead to life.

You probably wear black clothing, which might be adorned with skulls, bones, teeth, or other symbols of death. Some who consort with the dead paint their skin and dye their hair black, red, and white to bring them visually closer to the bodies they interact with.

Nanos are the most likely characters to consort with the dead, calling themselves "necromancers." Glaives and jacks who plumb these dark depths are sometimes referred to as "death warriors" or "death knights."

Connection: Choose one of the following.

1. Pick one other PC. You suspect that this character finds your predilections abhorrent. You can choose whether or not she knows of your suspicions.

2. Pick one other PC. This character recently lost a loved one and wants you to contact that person in the afterlife. Whether you try to explain that this isn't how it works is up to you.

3. Pick one other PC. This character looks upon you as some kind of religious figure (whether you encourage this behavior is up to you).

4. Pick one other PC. This character comes from the same place you do, and you knew each other as children.

Additional Equipment: You carry an innocuous memento of someone close to you who died. It might be a locket, a ring, a letter, a coin, or something similar.

Necromantic Esoteries: If you perform esoteries, those that would normally use force or other energy (such as electricity) instead use deathly energies. For example, your Flash esotery is a blast of cold, life-draining energy. This alteration changes nothing except that the type of damage is different, and it harms only living creatures.

Minor Effect Suggestions: The animated creature adds 1 to all rolls, or the target is dazed for one round, during which time the difficulty of all tasks it performs is modified by one step to its detriment.

Major Effect Suggestions: The animated creature adds 2 to all rolls, or the target is stunned and loses his next turn.

Tier 1: Speaker for the Dead (2+ Intellect points). You can ask a question of a dead being whose corpse you are touching. Because the answer comes through the filter of the being's understanding and personality, it can't answer questions that it wouldn't have understood in life, and it can't provide answers that it wouldn't have known in life. In fact, the being is not compelled to answer at all, so you might need to interact with it in a way that would have convinced it to answer while it was alive. For each additional Intellect point you spend when you activate the ability, you can ask the being an additional question. Action.

Tier 2: Necromancy (3+ Intellect points). You animate the body of a dead creature of approximately your size or smaller, creating a level 1 creature. It has none of the intelligence, memories, or special abilities that it had in life. The creature follows your verbal commands for one hour, after which it becomes an inert corpse. Unless the creature

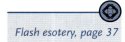
Flash esotery, page 37

is killed by damage, you can reanimate it again when its time expires, but any damage it had when it became inert applies to its newly reanimated state. If you have access to multiple bodies, you can create an additional undead creature for each additional Intellect point you spend when you activate the ability. Action to animate.

Tier 3: Reading the Room (3 Intellect points). You gain knowledge about an area by reading residual energies from the past. You can ask the GM a single, matter-of-fact question about the location and get an answer if you succeed on the Intellect roll. "What killed the cattle in this barn?" is a good example of a simple question. "Why were these cattle killed?" is not an appropriate question because it has more to do with the mindset of the killer than the barn. Simple questions usually have a difficulty of 2, but extremely technical questions or those that involve facts meant to be kept secret can have a much higher difficulty. Action.

Tier 4: Greater Necromancy (5+ Intellect points). This ability works like the second-tier Necromancy ability except that it creates a level 3 creature. Action to animate.

Tier 5: Death Gaze (6 Intellect points). You project a chilling gaze at all living creatures within short range who can see you. Make a separate Intellect attack roll for each target. Success means that the creature is frozen in fear, not moving or taking actions for one minute or until it is attacked. Some creatures without minds (such as automatons) might be immune to Death Gaze. Action.

Tier 6: True Necromancy (8+ Intellect points). This ability works like the second-tier Necromancy ability except that it creates a level 5 creature. Action to animate.

CONSTANTLY EVOLVES

Only mutant characters can use this focus. You were born different, with traits and abilities that no one else had. You embraced this nature, and through the use of training, drugs, radiation, and more you have continued to mutate your own body to develop new aspects of your strange biology.

If you don't have distinctive or cosmetic mutations, you might try to hide your nature to walk among "normal" people unnoticed. Or perhaps you flaunt your differences, daring

anyone to say or do anything about it. You likely enjoy the company of other mutants and probably study the different kinds of mutations (and causes of mutation) that exist.

Any character type can be a mutant and thus can constantly evolve. A mutant can come from any walk of life or any locale.

Connection: Choose one of the following.
1. Pick one other PC. This character seems put off by your nature as a mutant.
2. Pick one other PC. Although it is subtle, you suspect that this character might be a mutant with latent powers that she is not even aware of.
3. Pick two or more other PCs. You've decided not to let these characters know that you are a mutant. Instead, you tell them that your abilities are the result of something else: numenera devices, esoteries, or just simply magic.
4. Pick one other PC. You have found this character to be supportive and helpful, despite your mutant nature.

Additional Equipment: You have a variety of dangerous substances that you carefully expose yourself to in order to further your mutations.

Minor Effect Suggestions: The foe is startled by the sudden revelation of your mutations. The foe is dazed for one round, during which time the difficulty of all tasks it performs is modified by one step to its detriment.

Major Effect Suggestions: The foe is stunned and loses his next turn.

Tier 1: Improved Mutation. One mutation of your choice works better. You choose how it is modified (but choose something appropriate):
• The duration of the power is doubled.
• The range of the power is increased by one step (touch becomes immediate, immediate becomes short, short becomes long, and long becomes 200 feet [61 m]).
• It inflicts 3 additional points of damage.
• Work out something with the GM that is specific to the mutation.
Enabler.

Tier 2: New Mutation. You gain one new beneficial mutation, or two new beneficial mutations and one harmful mutation. Enabler.

Tier 3: Mutation Focus. Choose a mutation that you are not trained in. You are trained in the use of that mutation. Enabler.

Tier 4: Rework. You can undo the effects of one harmful mutation, but if you do, you gain

Consorts With the Dead GM Intrusions: *People who interact with the dead have frightening reputations. They might be outlawed in some places and hailed as saviors in others. Communicating with the spirits of dead aliens or other inhuman creatures can lead to madness.*

Constantly Evolves GM Intrusions: *Many people fear and hate mutants. Some powerful forces hunt them. Mutant powers sometimes get out of control or mutations spontaneously (and perhaps temporarily) harm the mutant.*

one cosmetic mutation.

Mutation Focus. Choose a mutation that you are not trained in. You are trained in the use of that mutation. Enabler.

Tier 5: New Mutation. You gain two new beneficial mutations, or three new beneficial mutations and a harmful mutation, or one new powerful mutation and one harmful mutation, or one new distinctive mutation and one harmful mutation. Enabler.

Tier 6: Mutation Specialization. Choose a mutation that you are trained in. You are specialized in the use of that mutation. Enabler.

DEFENDS THE WEAK

Someone has to stand up for the helpless, the weak, and the unprotected. You believe this duty, this obligation, falls to you, and thus you have spent much of your life watching out for the people around you. When you see them in trouble, you are the first to come to their aid. You might give up your last shin to help the hungry, take a beating to save a person from the same, or rally your friends to take on injustice wherever you find it.

You probably bear many scars from previous conflicts, but for each scar, you likely also have a token of gratitude. You may have a dried flower given to you by a lady you saved from brigands, or a bit of metal given to you by a starving man you fed.

Glaives typically take up the cause of the weak, having the grit, determination, and durability to face down dangerous threats. Jacks, however, may pursue these goals as vigilantes, while nanos bring to bear fabulous powers in the defense of others.

Connection: Choose one of the following.

1. Pick one other PC. You failed to protect this character at some point in the past, and you feel compelled to make up for your previous failure.

2. Pick one other PC. That character claimed innocence during a long-ago event, and you protected him. Now that time has passed, you're not entirely convinced that he was blameless.

3. Pick two other PCs. They seem to think that you are more of an arbitrator than you really are, and they keep asking you to choose which one of them is correct.

4. Pick one other PC. She believes that one of the tokens of gratitude you carry came from her father.

Additional Equipment: You have a shield.

Minor Effect Suggestions: You can draw an attack without having to use an action at any point before the end of the next round.

Major Effect Suggestions: You can take an extra action. You can use this action only to guard.

Tier 1: Courageous. You are trained in Intellect defense tasks and initiative tasks. Enabler.

Warding Shield. You have +1 to Armor while you are wielding a shield. Enabler.

Tier 2: Devoted Defender (2 Intellect points). Choose one character you can see. That character becomes your ward. You are trained in all tasks involving finding, healing, interacting with, and protecting that character. You can have only one ward at a time. Action to initiate.

Insight. You are trained in tasks to discern others' motives and to ascertain their general nature. You have a knack for sensing whether or not someone is truly innocent. Enabler.

Tier 3: True Guardian (2 Might points). When you stand guard as your action, you decrease the difficulty of all defense tasks by one step for characters you choose that are adjacent to you. This lasts until the end of your next turn. Enabler.

Tier 4: Combat Challenge. You are trained in intimidation tasks and in Intellect tasks made to draw an attack.

Willing Sacrifice. When you take an attack for another character, the attack does not deal 1 additional point of damage. Enabler.

Tier 5: Drive Back (4 Might points). When you deal damage with an attack, you can drive the creature away from your companions. Until the end of the next round, all characters other than you have an asset on Speed defense rolls made to resist attacks from this creature. Enabler.

Tier 6: True Defender (6 Intellect points). This ability functions as your Devoted Defender ability, except the benefit applies to up to three characters you choose. If you choose just one character, you become specialized in the tasks described under the Devoted Defender ability. Action to initiate.

EXISTS IN TWO PLACES AT ONCE

One day, you looked into a mirror or another

Defends the Weak GM Intrusions: A character focused on protecting others may periodically leave himself vulnerable to attacks.

Draw an attack, page 101
Take an attack, page 101

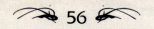

reflective surface and noticed that the reflection didn't quite match your movements. After some time, the image stepped free from the surface and where there was one, there were now two.

You have a doppelganger, a duplicate you can call into existence when you wish. This duplicate may be a quirk of your nature, brought on by exposure to weird energy or a piece of scarcely understood technology from the ancients. Then again, this other might hail from another reality, a branching timeline that may be similar to or quite different from your own. Of course, the copy could simply be a manifestation of your will on a cloud of nanites that assume your shape when you command them. Whatever the reason for your ability, you can call forth the copy and be in two places at once.

Your duplicate is your twin. It shares more than your appearance. It duplicates your mannerisms, manner of speech, expressions, and habits. In effect, you have another you.

Nanos are the most likely to have this unusual talent, for they dabble in forces most people cannot begin to understand. Glaives and jacks, however, often find themselves in strange places and encounter weird energies and may find the capabilities offered by this focus useful in pursuit of their goals.

Connection: Choose one of the following.

1. Pick one other PC. This character finds your talent unnerving and unsettling. For her, the difficulty of any task made to help your duplicate is increased by one step.

2. Pick one other PC. This character seems convinced that you are really a pair of identical twins with no actual powers.

3. Pick one other PC with a companion. This PC's companion seems to have an unusual relationship with your duplicate.

4. Pick one other PC. You used to move in the same social circles and knew of each other, but you had never been introduced.

Four Hands Are Better Than Two: When you and your duplicate work together to complete a task, the difficulty of that task is decreased by one step (if cooperation would be helpful).

Minor Effect Suggestions: For your target, the difficulty of the next task it attempts involving you or your duplicate before the end of the next round is increased by one step.

Major Effect Suggestions: You have an asset on the next roll you make within the next hour.

Tier 1: Duplicate (2 Might points). You cause a duplicate of yourself to appear at any point you

can see within short range. The duplicate has no clothing or possessions when it appears. The duplicate is a level 2 nonplayer character with 6 health. The duplicate obeys your commands and does as you direct it. The duplicate remains until you dismiss it using an action or until it is killed. When the duplicate disappears, it leaves behind anything it was wearing or carrying at the time it disappeared. If the duplicate disappears because it was killed, you take 4 points of damage that ignore Armor, and you lose your next action. Action to initiate.

Tier 2: Share Senses. While your duplicate is in existence and within 1 mile (1.6 km), you know everything it experiences and can communicate with it telepathically. Enabler.

Tier 3: Superior Duplicate (2 Might points). When you use your Duplicate ability, you can create a superior duplicate instead of a normal duplicate. A superior duplicate is a level 3 nonplayer character with 15 health. Enabler.

Tier 4: Damage Transference. When you or your duplicate would take damage, you can transfer 1 point of damage from one to the other provided that you and your duplicate are within 1 mile (1.6 km) of each other. Enabler.

Tier 5: Coordinated Effort (3 Intellect points). When you and your duplicate would attack the same creature, you can choose to make one attack roll with an asset. If you hit, you inflict damage with both attacks and treat the attacks as if they were one attack for the purpose of subtracting Armor from the damage. Action.

Resilient Duplicate. Increase the health of any duplicate you create by 5.

Tier 6: Multiplicity (6 Might points). This ability functions as Duplicate, except you can create two duplicates. Action to initiate.

EXPLORES DEEP WATERS

You have nothing to fear from the depths. You have always been a good swimmer, being able to hold your breath longer than anyone else, tread water for as long as you wanted, and delve deeper into the swirling darkness than your friends, all without stretching your resources. The depths you so freely explore harbor many secrets, and the waters that shelter you become part of who you are, an extension of your identity.

When you bother to wear clothes, you favor

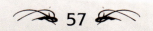

Onslaught, page 35

Redfleets, page 226
Jaekels of Aras Island,
page 169

snug, tight-fitting garments that stay close to your skin and do not hamper your mobility.

Jacks, being versatile and adaptable, are the most likely to explore deep waters, though anyone can choose this focus. The abilities it grants might result from special equipment you make along the way, weird transformations that began when you first swam into the deepest, darkest places, or simply an expression of an unusual gift.

Connection: Choose one of the following.

1. Pick one other PC. That character nearly drowned while following you on one of your expeditions underwater. The character's player can decide whether his PC would trust you in such an environment again.

2. Pick one other PC. She knows something about your past (possibly with the Redfleets) that you wish she didn't.

3. Pick one other PC. He suspects that you were involved with pirates—perhaps even with the Jaekels of Aras Island. Whether you were or not is up to you.

4. Pick one other PC. She can't swim very well and fears open water. You believe that you can help her overcome these issues, if she is willing to let you.

Additional Equipment: You have a special oddity that, when fitted in your mouth, allows you to breathe underwater. The device functions for up to four hours at a time, after which you must wait four hours before you can use it again.

Water Esoteries: If you perform esoteries, those that would normally use force or other

energy instead use water or ice. For example, Onslaught might create a wave of water that crashes down on your target.

In addition, you can swap out one of the esoteries you learned for the following.

Create Water (2 Intellect points). You cause water to bubble up from a spot on the ground you can see. The water flows from that spot for one minute, creating about 1 gallon (3.8 liters) by the time it stops.

Minor Effect Suggestions: You can take an extra action. You may use this action only to move or perform a movement-related activity.

Major Effect Suggestions: The difficulty of any Speed defense actions you make before the end of the next round is reduced by one step.

Tier 1: Diver. You can safely dive into water from heights of up to 100 feet (30 m), and you can withstand pressure when in water as deep as 100 feet (30 m). Enabler.

Hold Breath. You can hold your breath for up to five minutes. Enabler.

Trained Swimmer. While underwater, you are trained in escaping, perception, sneaking, and swimming tasks, as well as in tasks to identify aquatic creatures and geography. Enabler.

Tier 2: Eyes Adjusted. You can see in extremely dim light as though it were bright light. You can see in total darkness as if it were extremely dim light. Enabler.

Resist Underwater Hazards. Whether you're resisting the crushing waters from exploring the depths or a sting from a poisonous fish, the difficulty of all defense actions while submerged in water is reduced by one step. Enabler.

Tier 3: Aquatic Combatant. You ignore penalties for any action (including fighting) in underwater environments. Enabler.

Athletic Conditioning. Your Might Pool and Speed Pool each increase by 1 point. Enabler.

Tier 4: Nimble Swimmer. You are trained in all defense actions made while underwater. Enabler.

Swim (1+ Intellect points). You can swim like a fish through water and similar liquid for one hour. For each level of Effort applied, you can extend the duration by one hour. You swim about 10 miles (16 km) per hour, and you are not affected by currents in the water. Action to initiate.

Tier 5: Communication (2 Intellect Points). You can convey a basic concept or ask a simple question to a creature that lives underwater and cannot speak or understand speech, and the creature can provide you with a basic answer. Action.

Elusive (2 Speed points). When you succeed on a Speed defense action, you immediately gain an action. You can use this action only to move. Enabler.

Tier 6: Deep Water Guide. While underwater, any creature you choose that can see you has an asset on swimming tasks. Enabler.

Master of the Deep Waters. While underwater, your Might Edge, Speed Edge, and Intellect Edge each increase by 1. Enabler.

Water Adaptation. You can breathe water as easily as you breathe air. Enabler.

FIGHTS DIRTY

You know one thing for certain: the only important element of a fight is who wins. How? Why? These questions are inconsequential. Thus, you'll do anything to win a fight. Some might say you have no honor, no class, or some other foolish statement, but they're missing the point. You come out on top in a battle—and that's all that matters.

You bite, scratch, kick, and trip. You tangle foes in draperies, push them down stairs, and throw dirt in their eyes. You trick them into looking the wrong way, call them names, and say terrible things about their mothers.

Maybe you learned your methods while living in the streets, or maybe you barely survived a particularly horrific battle in a military campaign. Perhaps you simply have never bought into the idea of rules or honor when your life is on the line.

You're likely to carry a few hidden tricks, sometimes literally up your sleeve. You might have a knife in your boot, a poisoned needle in your ring, a razor in the hem of your cloak, or a handful of stinging and itching powder in a hidden pocket. Your clothing probably has a lot of pockets, actually—more than a few of them well hidden.

Glaives and jacks are most often dirty fighters, but a scrappy nano who isn't afraid to get into the thick of things and use esoteries to enhance her tricks would make a fine dirty fighter.

Connection: Choose one of the following.

1. Pick one other PC. He's a good fighter, but if you could teach him a few of your tricks, he'd really excel.

2. Pick one other PC. In the past, she taught you a few tricks to use in a fight.

Fights Dirty GM Intrusions: *People look poorly upon those who fight without honor or "cheat." Sometimes a dirty trick backfires, and you end up with a handful of dirt in your eyes instead.*

3. Pick one other PC. This character doesn't seem to approve of your methods.

4. Pick one other PC. Long ago, the two of you were on opposite sides of a fight. You won, using your particular tactics. Now she's clearly interested in a (friendly) rematch at some point and claims to be ready for you.

Additional Equipment: You have a weapon that is easily hidden and a dose of level 3 poison that inflicts 6 points of damage.

Minor Effect Suggestions: You manage to make your foe trip and fall prone.

Major Effect Suggestions: You tangle something around your foe's legs, and he not only falls down but also loses his next turn.

Tier 1: Taking Advantage. When your foe is weakened, dazed, stunned, moved down the damage track, or disadvantaged in some other way, the difficulty of your attacks against that foe is decreased by one step beyond any other modifications due to the disadvantage. Enabler.

Lattimor, page 122
Bursk, page 122
Neem, page 122

Liar. You are trained in all forms of deception. Enabler.

Tier 2: Eye Gouge (2 Speed points). You make an attack against a creature with an eye. The difficulty of the attack is increased by one step, but if you hit, the creature has trouble seeing for the next hour. During this time, the difficulty of any of the creature's tasks that rely upon sight (which is most tasks) is increased by one step.

Tier 3: Spot Weakness. If a creature that you can see has a special weakness, such as a particular vulnerability to fire, a negative modification to perception, or so on, you know what it is. (Ask and the GM will tell you.) Enabler.

Betrayal. Any time you convince a foe that you are not a threat and then suddenly attack them (without provocation), the attack deals 4 additional points of damage. Enabler.

Tier 4: Mind Games (3 Intellect points). You use lies and trickery against a foe that can understand you. If successful, the foe is stunned for one round and cannot act, and the foe is dazed on the following round, during which time the difficulty of all of the foe's tasks is increased by one step.

Tooth and Nail. If, during a melee combat, you are willing to literally bite and claw at a foe in addition to attacking with your normal weapon, you inflict 1 additional point of damage each time you strike with your standard attack. Some creatures (such as automatons or incorporeal creatures) might not be subject to this, and attempting to bite some creatures might be dangerous. Enabler.

Tier 5: Using the Environment (4 Intellect points). You find some way to use the environment to your advantage in a fight. For the next ten minutes, the difficulty of attack rolls and Speed defense rolls is decreased by one step. Action to initiate.

Tier 6: Twisting the Knife (4 Speed points). On a round after successfully striking a foe with a melee weapon, you can opt to automatically deal standard damage to the foe with that same weapon without any modifiers (2 points for a light weapon, 4 points for a medium weapon, or 6 points for a heavy weapon). Action.

FOCUSES TWO PERSONALITIES
Only lattimor characters can use this focus. Lattimors are symbiotic entities. Their very existence lies at the confluence of the bursk and

the neem. A few lattimors learn to bring together these two disparate entities, creating a more unified fugue state that capitalizes on bursk strength and neem willpower. At the same time, however, the two personalities are not lessened, but rather enhanced. While the whole may be greater than the sum of its parts, the parts are heightened as the whole advances.

You are a lattimor who focuses both your personalities to make each state—bursk, neem, and fugue—greater. To most others, these changes are likely not noticeable. However, to those who know what to look for, the differences are remarkable. You display more of the strengths of each personality within the fugue state, and you shift through your states much faster.

Connection: Choose one of the following.

1. Pick two other non-lattimor PCs. Each of these characters is close friends with your bursk state or neem state, but not both.

2. Pick one other PC. When this character is within close range, either your bursk state or your neem state gets a +1 bonus to all rolls, but the other state suffers a –1 penalty to all rolls.

3. Pick one other PC. This character seems to have gone out of her way to gain an understanding of lattimor psychology and physiology.

4. Pick one other non-lattimor PC. This character was one of the first non-lattimors you ever got to know.

Minor Effect Suggestions: You knock your foe off its feet with your strength and size.

Major Effect Suggestions: Even as you attack with your bursk sensibilities, you size up your foe with your neem focus. The difficulty of your next attack against the foe is decreased by two steps.

Tier 1: Greater Fugue State. In addition to being trained in perception, while in fugue state you are also trained in breaking things and all interactions with others. Enabler.

Easier Change. The default difficulty of changing your state is 2 instead of 4. Enabler.

Tier 2: Two Minds. You are trained in Intellect defense tasks. Enabler.

Mind–Body Efficiency. You have 6 additional points to permanently divide among your stat Pools. Enabler.

Tier 3: Easier Change. The default difficulty of changing your state is 0. You can change as often as you desire. Enabler.

Fighting Fugue State. While in your fugue state, you are trained in the same attacks that you have selected for your bursk state. Enabler.

Tier 4: Both at Once (5 Intellect points). You can take two actions in one round, one in your bursk state and one in your neem state. Enabler.

Tier 5: Exacerbation. While in bursk state, you inflict 3 additional points of damage with melee weapons. While in neem state, the difficulty of all Intellect-based actions is decreased by one step. Enabler.

Tier 6: Mind–Body Efficiency. You have 6 additional points to permanently divide among your stat Pools. Enabler.

Easier Change. It is no longer an action to change state, but you cannot change more than once each round. Enabler.

FUSES MIND AND MACHINE

You believe that the finest machine ever created is the human brain (although some experts of the numenera would disagree). Experience and training have taught you that any machine can be improved. Through the use of implants and mechanical enhancements, your brain processes input faster, stores more information, and eventually can tap right into the datasphere. Mentally, you function on an entirely different level than your fellows.

Did you make these improvements yourself? Did someone else? Was it with your blessing or against your will? Regardless, you are now more than just a person. You are both living creature and machine. But unlike what others might assume, all of your numenera refinements and upgrades are on the inside. You don't need mech eyes or metal arms to be enhanced. It's all about what's inside your skull.

Nanos are most often those who fuse their mind with machines.

Connection: Choose one of the following.

1. Pick one other PC. This character knows a few things that can help when your implants and enhancements malfunction.

2. Pick one other PC. He seems to find you off-putting. You wonder if it's because you're clearly smarter than he is or if it's for some other reason entirely.

3. Pick one other PC. This character has a small device that can shut down your brain with a single switch. However, you don't think he has any idea of what it is or what it can do.

4. Pick one other PC. Within your memory

Focuses Two Personalities GM Intrusions: *Bickering personalities can lead to lost actions.*

Fuses Mind and Machine GM Intrusions: *Machines malfunction and shut down. Powerful machine intelligences can take control of lesser thinking machines. Some people don't trust a person who isn't fully organic.*

circuits, you have data of someone who looks just like that character committing terrible crimes—hundreds of years ago. You have no explanation.

Additional Equipment: You have an artifact that protects your implants and enhancements from disruption or intrusion. The difficulty of resisting such attacks is decreased by one step.

Minor Effect Suggestions: You foresee your foes' moves so well that the difficulty of Speed defense rolls for the next round is decreased by one step.

Major Effect Suggestions: Processing surge! On your next action, you can use points from your Intellect Pool rather than your Might or Speed Pools.

Tier 1: Mechanical Assistance. You gain 4 additional points to your Intellect Pool through the use of implants and tiny processing devices. Enabler.

Stored Memories: You are trained in one area of knowledge (history, geography, astronomy, and so on) of your choice. Enabler.

Tier 2: Datasphere Tap (4 Intellect points). You can ask the GM one question and get a very short answer. Action.

Tier 3: Action Processor (4 Intellect points). Drawing upon stored information and the ability to process incoming data at amazing speeds, you are trained in one physical task of your choice for ten minutes. For example, you can choose running, climbing, swimming, Speed defense, or even attacks with a specific weapon. Action to initiate.

Tier 4: Processing Power. You gain 2 additional points to your Intellect Pool and 1 additional point to your Intellect Edge. Enabler.

More Stored Memories: You are trained in one area of knowledge (history, geography, astronomy, and so on) of your choice. Enabler.

Tier 5: See the Future (6 Intellect points). Based on all the variables you perceive, you can predict the next few minutes. This has the following effects:

• For the next ten minutes, the difficulty of all your defense rolls is reduced by one step.

• You have a sort of "danger sense." For the next ten minutes, you can predict the actions of those around you. You are trained in seeing through deceptions and attempts to betray you as well as avoiding traps and ambushes.

• You know what people are probably thinking and what they will say before they say it. You are trained in all skills involving interaction and deception. Enabler.

Tier 6: Reboot. In addition to your normal recovery rolls each day, you can—at any time between ten-hour rests—recover 1d6 + 6 points to your Intellect Pool. Action.

Enhancement. Any time you use Effort on an Intellect action, add one of the following enhancements to the action (your choice):

• +2 to the roll
• +2 to damage
• Automatic minor effect
Enabler.

HUNTS ABHUMANS

Abhumans are a threat to humanity. You know this more than anyone. The threat is obvious—bestial abhumans attack villages, caravans, and travelers all the time in the wilderness. But the threat is also far more subtle. The progenitors of the abhumans were once human. They gave up their humanity to become horrific, monstrous things ages ago. How this happened, or how long ago—these are things you cannot conceive. But you know that they are true, so abhumans must be eradicated for the good of all.

Abhuman hunters are usually glaives who wear tough but practical armor and carry a wide variety of weapons. But a jack or nano could join their ranks as well, becoming decidedly more warriorlike than their fellows. Regardless, abhuman hunters spend much of their time stalking through the wastelands and desolate wilds as well as guarding what few roads and paths connect the towns and villages of the Ninth World.

Connection: Choose one of the following.

1. Pick one other PC. This character has had experiences with abhumans in the past, and you'd like to know more about them.

2. Pick one other PC. You are friends, and you'd hate to see this character harmed.

3. Pick one other PC. This character doesn't understand just how dangerous and horrible abhumans can be.

4. Pick one other PC. Abhumans are sometimes drawn to certain people. They always seem to attack those people first and with more fervor. This character appears to be one such person.

Minor Effect Suggestions: Your foe is so intimidated by your prowess that it backs away, unwilling to attack. It can still defend itself.

Major Effect Suggestions: Your foe is terrified by your skill and flees.

Tier 1: Tracker and Hunter. When tracking, looking for, interacting with, or hiding from abhumans, the difficulty of the task is decreased by one step. Enabler.

Abhuman Fighter. You inflict 2 additional points of damage when fighting abhumans. Enabler.

Tier 2: Abhuman Sense (2 Intellect points). Through scent, specific signs, and past experience, you know when abhumans are within long range for one hour. Enabler.

Expert Combatant. Choose one type of attack in which you are not already trained:

Hunts Abhumans GM Intrusions:

Abhumans are often smart enough to take out the biggest threat first. They sometimes make surprising use of poison, traps, and ambushes.

light bashing, light bladed, light ranged, medium bashing, medium bladed, medium ranged, heavy bashing, heavy bladed, or heavy ranged. You are trained in attacks using that type of weapon. Enabler.

Tier 3: Horde Fighting. When two or more foes attack you at once in melee, you can use them against each other. The difficulty of Speed defense rolls or attack rolls (your choice) against them is reduced by one step. Enabler.

Tier 4: **Improved Abhuman Fighter.** You inflict 3 additional points of damage when fighting abhumans. Enabler.

Tier 5: Abhuman Slayer. When fighting abhumans, the difficulty of all attack rolls and defense rolls is decreased by one step. Enabler.

Tier 6: Master Combatant. Choose one type of attack in which you are already trained: light bashing, light bladed, light ranged, medium bashing, medium bladed, medium ranged, heavy bashing, heavy bladed, or heavy ranged. You are specialized in attacks using that type of weapon. Enabler.

HUNTS MUTANTS

Mutants represent everything that is wrong with your world. They are a scourge upon humanity. They are a disease that must be put down. You don't necessarily take pleasure in that—you don't relish their eradication. But it must be done for the good of the human race. If this malady is not destroyed now, it will only spread to future generations, and in greater numbers.

You very likely have had experiences with mutants in your past. You know that not every mutant is a hideous monstrosity. However, you also know that mutants who are not obvious typically pose the greatest threat because they can hide in plain sight.

As a mutant hunter, you know that it takes special tools to fight creatures with crazy powers and abilities. You have learned to adapt devices to aid in finding mutants and defending yourself against them. This might mean imbibing or injecting chemicals, nanites, or other strange treatments to even the odds.

Jacks, with their wide range of abilities, often make the best mutant hunters.

Connection: Choose one of the following.

1. Pick one other PC. You believe that this character might hate and fear mutants as much as you do (although it's up to that character's player as to whether this is true).

2. Pick one other PC. In the past, when you were with this character, she was harmed by a mutant, which helped inspire you to hunt them in the first place.

3. Pick one other PC. This character seems to believe that mutants should be left in peace.

4. Pick one other PC. You worry that this character might be a latent mutant.

Additional Equipment: You have a small collection of items, such as chemicals and nanites, that you believe aid you as you hunt and destroy mutants.

Minor Effect Suggestions: Your foe is so intimidated by your prowess that it backs away, unwilling to attack. It can still defend itself.

Major Effect Suggestions: Your foe is disrupted and off balance and can't use any special powers that require an action for two rounds.

Tier 1: Mutant Fighter. You inflict 3 additional points of damage when fighting mutants. Enabler.

Tier 2: Mutant Tracker (2+ Intellect points). You can sense the presence of a mutant within long range. Once you have found a specific mutant, if you then use a level of Effort, you can attempt to "lock on" to it. If you succeed, you always know the distance and direction to it. Enabler.

Tier 3: Defense Against Mutant Powers. Mutant powers can come in many forms. You are trained in all types of defense. Enabler.

Tier 4: Mutation Disruption (4 Intellect points). One mutant you touch cannot access any of the benefits of its mutations for ten minutes. Action.

Tier 5: Fire With Fire. Through the use of nanites, drugs, or biomechanical alterations, you give yourself abilities. You gain two beneficial "mutations," or three beneficial "mutations" and a harmful "mutation," or one powerful "mutation" and one harmful "mutation," or one distinctive "mutation" and one harmful "mutation." You're always quick to point out that these modifications are not truly mutations. Enabler.

Hunts Mutants GM Intrusions: *Mutants might begin hunting the hunter. Mutants sometimes manifest powers that they didn't know they had. Sometimes you just can't tell if a person is a mutant.*

Tier 6: True Defense Against Mutant Powers. Mutant powers can come in many forms. You are specialized in all types of defense.

MASTERS INSECTS

You are a master of the hive mind, controller of those with compound eyes, friend to all that fly and flitter. It's a weird skill—as you've been told far too many times—but you've seen the benefits both in and out of battle, and you've fully embraced it.

Your dress likely bears some mark of your predilections. Perhaps you use goldgleam or other insectoid elements to adorn yourself, or perhaps your cloth is the rainbow hue of a beetle's back. Butterflies and other insects sometimes alight on your person even when you don't purposefully call them.

The masters of insects are most often nanos simply because dealing with insects is mentally taxing, and they are usually the characters best able to cope. These nanos are sometimes called swarm lords.

Connection: Choose one of the following.

1. Pick one other PC. This person seems deathly afraid of some or all kinds of insects and has a watchful eye on you.

2. Pick one other PC. Your insects are attracted to this person for reasons you cannot understand.

3. Pick one other PC. You are indebted to this character for an act of kindness in the past.

4. Pick one other PC. This character has an insect-shaped birthmark, mole, or other feature. Does it mean something?

Additional Equipment: You have an oddity that makes random insect noises when you press a button.

Minor Effect Suggestions: The insect swarm is particularly thick and angry, and everyone within it suffers 1 point of damage this round.

Major Effect Suggestions: Everyone within the insect swarm suffers 3 points of damage this round.

Tier 1: Influence Insects (1 Intellect point). Insects within short range will not harm you or those you designate as allies for one hour. Action to initiate.

Tier 2: Control Insects (2 Intellect points). Insects within short range do as you telepathically command for ten minutes. Even common insects (level 0) in large enough numbers can swarm about a single creature and modify its task difficulty by one step to its detriment. Action to initiate.

Goldgleam, page 180

Masters Insects GM Intrusions: *You might think you have perfect control of the hive mind, but that's not always how it works. Telepathic connections break. A swarm receives an incorrect signal. Accidental stings or bites occur.*

Insect swarms don't typically have game stats, but if needed, a typical swarm is level 2. Only attacks that affect a large area affect the swarm.

Tier 3: Insect Armor (4 Intellect points). If you're in a location where it's possible for insects to come, you call a swarm of insects around you for one hour. They crawl over your body and fly around you in a cloud. During this time, the difficulty of Speed defense tasks is decreased by one step, and you gain +1 to Armor. Action to initiate.

Tier 4: Call Swarm (4 Intellect points). If you're in a location where it's possible for insects to come, you call a swarm of common insects to you that remain for one hour. During this hour, they do as you telepathically command as long as they are within long range. They can swarm about and modify any or all creatures' task difficulties by one step to their detriment. While the insects are in long range, you can speak to them telepathically and perceive through their senses. Action to initiate.

Tier 5: Insect Companion. You gain a flying insect as a constant companion. It is level 4, probably the size of a small dog, and follows your telepathic commands. You and the GM must work out the details of your creature, and you'll probably make rolls for it in combat or when it takes actions. The insect companion acts on your turn. As a

level 4 creature, it has a target number of 12 and a health of 12, and it inflicts 4 points of damage. If your insect companion dies, you can hunt in the wild for 1d6 days to find a new companion. Enabler.

Tier 6: Deadly Swarm (6 Intellect points). You call a swarm of insects in a place where it is possible for insects to come. They remain for ten minutes, and during this time, they do as you telepathically command as long as they are within long range. They can swarm about and modify any or all creatures' task difficulties by one step to their detriment, or they can focus the swarm and attack all creatures within immediate range of each other (all within long range of you). The attacking swarm inflicts 4 points of damage. While the insects are in long range, you can speak to them telepathically and perceive through their senses. Action to initiate.

METES OUT JUSTICE

So much injustice in the world. It takes a special person to take it upon himself to right wrongs, protect the innocent, and punish the guilty. You are such a person.

Justicars, as they are sometimes called,

are often knights errant who wear armor, bear swords and shields, and travel the land looking for tyranny, corruption, or oppression. But some operate a little less ostentatiously. Sometimes justice comes from more subtle tactics.

The importance of justice in your life might come from religion, your upbringing, or your highly developed sense of principles. Regardless, you not only adhere to your values, but you also believe it is your calling to act on them and help make the world more just, more fair, and more ethical. You want to see wrongdoing punished.

Although any character can be a justicar, glaives most often take on the role.

Connection: Choose one of the following.

1. Pick one other PC. You strongly suspect that this person has a past that might involve serious crimes or wrongdoing. You have no proof, however, and you've never witnessed him do anything seriously wrong.

2. Pick one other PC. This character seems to share your value systems and sees right and wrong the same way you do, which is refreshing.

3. Pick one other PC. This character, while ethical, defines right and wrong in different ways than you do.

4. Pick one other PC. In the past, you and this character witnessed an event that helped shape your moral code. She may or may not have come away with a similar outlook.

Additional Equipment: You have a shield to help you protect yourself and the innocents you find.

Minor Effect Suggestions: You shame or intimidate your foe so much that he is shaken and uses his next turn to flee.

Major Effect Suggestions: You mark your foe permanently with a distinctive scar so that her guilt will be known by all.

Tier 1: Make Judgment. You are skilled in discerning the truth of a situation, seeing through lies, or otherwise overcoming deception. Enabler.

Designation: You assign an "innocent" or "guilty" label to one creature within immediate range, based on your general assessment of a given situation or a predominant feeling. In other words, someone who is labeled "innocent" can be innocent in a certain circumstance, or he can be generally innocent of terrible crimes (such as murder, major theft, and so on). Likewise, you can declare that a creature is "guilty" of a particular crime or of terrible deeds

in general. The accuracy of your assessment isn't important as long as you believe it to be the truth; the GM may require you to give a rationale. Henceforth, the difficulty of tasks to socially interact with someone you designate as innocent is decreased by one step, and the difficulty of attacks against those you designate as guilty is decreased by one step. You can change your assessment, but it requires another designation action. The benefits of the designation last until you change it or until you are shown proof that it is wrong. Action.

Tier 2: Defend the Innocent (2 Speed points). For the next ten minutes, if someone you have designated as an innocent stands next to you, that creature shares any defensive advantages that you might have, other than mundane armor. These advantages include the Speed defense from your shield, the Armor offered from a force field, and so on. In addition, the difficulty of Speed defense rolls made by the innocent creature is decreased by one step. You can protect only one innocent creature at a time. Action to initiate.

Tier 3: Punish the Guilty (2 Might points). For the next ten minutes, if you attack someone you have designated as guilty, you inflict 2 additional points of damage. Action to initiate.

Tier 4: Find the Guilty. If you have designated someone as guilty, you are trained in tracking him, spotting him when he is hidden, or otherwise finding him. Enabler.

Greater Designation: You can assign an "innocent" or "guilty" label (as described above) to all creatures within immediate range. Action.

Tier 5: Punish All the Guilty (3 Speed points). You can attack all foes within immediate range that you have designated as guilty. Make separate attack rolls for each foe, but all attacks count as a single action in a single round. You remain limited by the amount of Effort you can apply on one action. Anything that modifies your attack or damage applies to all attacks. Action.

Tier 6: Defend All the Innocent. You protect everyone within immediate range who you have designated as innocent. The difficulty of Speed defense rolls made by such creatures is decreased by one step. Enabler.

Metes Out Justice GM Intrusions: *Guilt or innocence can be complicated. Some people resent the presumption of a self-appointed judge. Passing judgment makes enemies.*

**Moves Like a Cat
GM Intrusions:** *Even
a cat can be clumsy
sometimes, especially
when overconfident. A
well-calculated jump
isn't quite as easy as it
looks. An escape move
is so overzealous that
it sends the character
right into harm's way.*

Tier 1: Reflexes. You gain 3 additional points to your Speed Pool. Enabler.
   Balance. You are trained in balancing. Enabler.

Tier 2: Movement. You are trained in climbing and jumping. Enabler.
   Safe Fall. You reduce the damage from a fall by 5 points. Enabler.

Tier 3: Greater Reflexes. You gain 1 additional point to your Speed Edge. Enabler.
   Hard to Touch. You are trained in Speed defense tasks. Enabler.

Tier 4: Quick Strike (4 Speed points). You make a melee attack with such speed that it is hard for your foe to defend against, and it knocks him off balance. The difficulty of making the attack is decreased by two steps, and the foe, if struck, is dazed so that for the next round, the difficulty of all of his tasks is increased by one step. Action.

Tier 5: **Phenomenal Reflexes.** You gain 5 additional points to your Speed Pool.
   Slippery: You are trained in escaping any kind of bond or grasp.

Tier 6: Burst of Action (6 Speed points). You can take two separate actions this round. Enabler.

MOVES LIKE A CAT
You are extremely dexterous. Your speed and agility make you almost a thing of wonder. Your body is lithe, flexible, and graceful. Your training—or perhaps a bit of the numenera—allows you to move quickly and smoothly, land safely when you fall, and avoid danger.

You likely wear tight clothing that doesn't hinder you as you move. Likewise, you probably don't allow yourself to be overburdened by a lot of equipment. You'll wear armor only if it doesn't slow you down.

Glaives are very often catlike, but so are jacks.
   Connection:
   1. Pick one other PC. Their occasional clumsiness and loud behavior irritates you.
   2. Pick one other PC. This character comes from the same place you do, and you knew each other as children.
   3. Pick one other PC. You aid her with advice and a helping hand when she needs it. Anytime the two of you are next to each other, the difficulty of balancing, climbing, and jumping tasks is decreased by one step for her.
   4. Pick one other PC. He owes you 10 shins.
   Minor Effect Suggestions: You restore 2 points to your Speed Pool.
   Major Effect Suggestions: You can take a second action this round.

**Needs No Weapons
GM Intrusions:**
*Striking certain foes
hurts you as much as it
hurts them. Opponents
with weapons have
greater reach.
Complicated martial
arts moves can knock
you off balance.*

NEEDS NO WEAPON
You don't use weapons—you *are* a weapon. With powerful punches, kicks, and full-body moves, you inflict incredible damage on your foes. By focusing your energy, the combined power of your body and mind means you can do incredible amounts of damage without depleting your energy reserves. You might have gained your skills through intense training, various implants and enhancements, genetic mutations, or any combination of these things. Whatever the origin of your feats, you likely take good care of your body, ensuring that it remains the sharpest, most dependable weapon at your disposal.

Martial artists or kasundas (as those with your training are sometimes called) are both feared and revered. They wear loose, comfortable clothing that allows them a full range of movement, and they rarely use weapons other than their body's own implements (although some carry items designed to enhance their body movements

for greater effect, such as knuckle weapons, knee spikes, or boot blades).

Glaives are perhaps best suited for using their bodies as weapons, but jacks are also good candidates.

Connection: Choose one of the following.

1. Pick one other PC. He seems to believe that the only true weapons are those that you can hold in your hand, and he might look at you with disdain.

2. Pick one other PC. This person seems incredibly unaware of her body and always happens to get in your way. If you miss your foe and accidentally hit someone else in close range, it's likely to be her.

3. Pick one other PC. You once trained with a close friend of his, and you owe that mutual friend much.

4. Pick two other PCs. Once these two heard about your skills, they expressed interest in being your students. However, only one seems to have any aptitude.

Minor Effect Suggestions: You trip your target and knock him prone.

Major Effect Suggestions: You strike your target in a limb, making that limb useless for the next minute.

Tier 1: Fists of Fury. You inflict 2 additional points of damage with unarmed attacks. Enabler.

Flesh of Stone: You have +1 to Armor if you do not wear physical armor. Enabler.

Tier 2: Advantage to Disadvantage (2 Speed points). With a number of quick moves, you make an attack against a foe wielding a weapon, inflicting damage and disarming him so that his weapon is now 10 feet (3 m) away on the ground, or in your hands—your choice. The difficulty of the attack is increased by one step. Action.

Fighting Style: You are trained in unarmed attacks. Enabler.

Tier 3: Moving Like Water (3 Speed points). You spin and move so that your defense and attacks are aided by your fluid motion. For one minute, the difficulty of your attacks and Speed defense rolls is decreased by one step.

Tier 4: Deflect Attacks (4 Speed points). For one minute, you automatically deflect or dodge any ranged projectile attacks. However, during this time, the difficulty of all other actions in any round where you are attacked by ranged projectiles is increased by one step. Action to initiate.

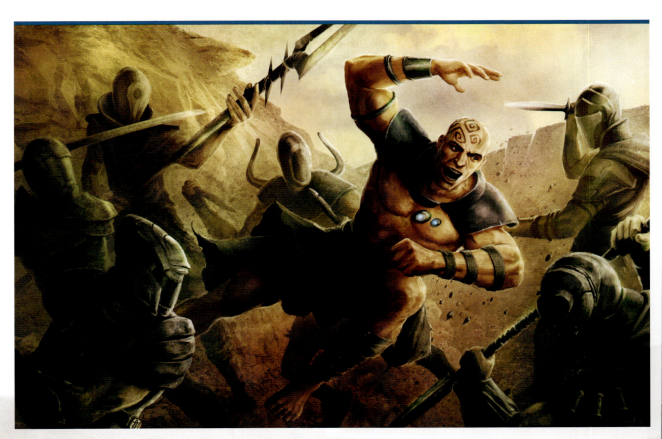

Tier 5: Stunning Attack (4 Might points). You hit your foe in just the right spot, stunning him so that he loses his next action. This attack inflicts no damage.

Tier 6: Master of Style. You are specialized in unarmed attacks. If you are already specialized in unarmed attacks, you instead deal 2 additional points of damage with unarmed attacks. Enabler.

NEVER SAYS DIE

You are as stalwart, hardy, and driven as can be imagined. When others are ready to quit, you're just getting started.

You probably don't spend a lot of time on your appearance—it is far less important than actions. For that matter, so are words. You're likely not much of a talker. You're a doer.

Characters with this focus are sometimes called stalwarts or diehards. They often are soldiers, mercenaries, or other tough-as-nails individuals, but sometimes they take a more heroic stance. A character who is hard to kill is around longer to help others, after all.

Stalwarts are most often glaives, but nanos who like to stand at the back of the pack out of harm's way can do serious damage as diehards.

Never Says Die GM Intrusions:

Even if you never give out, sometimes your equipment or weapons do.

Connection: Choose one of the following.

1. Pick one other PC. You feel the overwhelming need to impress this character, although you're not sure why.

2. Pick one other PC. This character seems quite capable, but in your mind, his spirit needs motivating. You're constantly trying to convince him to keep trying, go the distance, and keep fighting the good fight.

3. Pick one other PC. You feel very protective of this character and don't want to see her harmed.

4. Pick one other PC. This character comes from the same place you do, and you knew each other as children.

Minor Effect Suggestions: You restore 2 points to your Might Pool.

Major Effect Suggestions: The difficulty of your next action is decreased by two steps.

Tier 1: Rapid Recovery. Your ten-minute recovery roll period takes one action instead, so that your first two periods are one action, the third is one hour, and the fourth is ten hours. Enabler.

Push on Through (2 Might points). You ignore the effects of terrain while moving for one hour. Enabler.

Tier 2: Ignore the Pain. You ignore the impaired condition and treat the debilitated condition as impaired. Enabler.

Tier 3: Hidden Reserves. When you make a one-action recovery roll, you also gain 1 to your Might Edge and Speed Edge for ten minutes thereafter. Enabler.

Tier 4: Increasing Determination. If you fail at a noncombat physical task and then retry the task (pushing open a door or climbing a cliff, for example), the difficulty of the task is reduced by one step. If you fail again, you gain no special benefits. Enabler.

Outlast the Foe. If you have been in a combat for five full rounds, the difficulty of all tasks in the remainder of that combat is decreased by one step, and you deal 1 additional point of damage per attack. Enabler.

Tier 5: Throw off Affliction (5 Might points). If you are affected by an unwanted condition or affliction (such as disease, paralysis, mind control, broken limb, and so on, but not damage), you can ignore it and act as if it does not affect you for one hour. If the condition would normally last less than an hour, it is entirely negated. Action.

Tier 6: Not Dead Yet. When you would normally be dead, you fall unconscious for one round and then awaken. You immediately gain 1d6 + 6 points to restore your stat Pools and are treated as if debilitated (which for you is like impaired, thanks to your Ignore the Pain ability) until you rest for ten hours. If you die again before you take your ten-hour recovery roll period, you are truly dead. Enabler.

PERFORMS FEATS OF STRENGTH

A lifetime of physical training rewards you with incredible power. Your muscles ripple beneath your skin, evident in your extraordinary build and frame, and you can do things others would not dream possible. You can haul incredible weight, hurl your body through the air, and punch your fist through doors.

Superior strength can manifest in many ways. You could have the physique of a bodybuilder, almost godlike in its perfection, or you might be a lumbering, hulking monster of a person, as heavy with fat as you are with muscle. Then again, you could be short and wiry, your strength belied by your slight frame.

Glaives are the most likely to perform feats of strength.

Connection: Choose one of the following.

1. Pick one other PC. You have been friends with this character for as long as you remember and often heed her advice and guidance.

2. Pick one other PC. For some reason—nerves, perhaps, or attraction—he makes you feel weak in the knees. You prefer if he stays out of immediate range when you're in combat.

3. Pick one other PC. You once carried him from combat after he was wounded. Whether he feels embarrassment, gratitude, or something else is up to him.

4. Pick two other PCs. They have a game where they ask you to perform harder and harder feats of strength. Whether you play along is up to you.

Additional Equipment: You have a heavy weapon.

Minor Effect Suggestions: You knock the creature to the ground.

Major Effect Suggestions: You send the creature flying through the air so that it lands on the ground in a heap 1d20 feet away from you.

Tier 1: Athlete. You are trained in carrying, climbing, jumping, and smashing. Enabler.

Strong. Your Might Edge increases by 1. Enabler.

Tier 2: Feat of Strength (1 Might point). The difficulty of any task that depends on brute force—such as smashing down a barred door, tearing open a locked container, lifting or moving a heavy object, or striking someone with a melee weapon—is decreased by one step. Enabler.

Tier 3: Iron Fist. Your unarmed attacks deal 4 points of damage. Enabler.

Throw (2 Might points). When you deal damage to a creature of your size or smaller with an unarmed attack, you can choose to throw that creature up to 1d20 feet away from you. The creature lands prone. Enabler.

Tier 4: Powerful. Your Might Pool increases by 5 points. Enabler.

Tier 5: Brute Strike (4 Might points). You deal 4 additional points of damage with all melee attacks until the end of the next round. Enabler.

Performs Feats of Strength GM Intrusions: *A strong character might not realize her own strength and accidentally damage or destroy a delicate object she handles.*

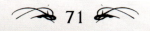

Possesses a Shard of the Sun GM Intrusions: *Sudden bright light can leave others dazzled or even blinded when you don't intend them to be.*

Ward, page 36

Tier 6: Juggernaut (5 Might points). Until the end of the next round, you can move through solid objects such as doors and walls. Only 2 feet (0.6 m) of wood, 1 foot (0.3 m) of stone, or 6 inches (15 cm) of metal can stop your movement. Enabler.

POSSESSES A SHARD OF THE SUN

You have the ability to create and sculpt light, to bend it away from you or gather it to use as a weapon. Perhaps a shard of a strange stone became embedded in your flesh and through it you can control light. Or you might have always had the gift, a freak talent handed down to you by the ancients.

Most people able to command light favor bright colors in their clothing since those colors reflect light rather than absorb it.

Nanos tend to be the ones who possess shards of the sun, calling themselves light bearers or sun savants. They find its power useful for exploration and personal protection. Jacks

appreciate how the abilities help them trick and elude foes, while glaives harness the power to destroy their enemies.

Connection: Choose one of the following.

1. Pick one other PC. You have a strong emotional connection to this character and when in his presence, you can change the color of the light you create.

2. Pick one other PC. She is especially perceptive to your light and occasionally your flashes leave her dazzled, increasing the difficulty of her defense actions by one step.

3. Pick one other PC. Something about his nature dampens the light. Your light-based powers cost 1 additional Intellect point if he stands immediately next to you.

4. Pick one other PC. This character appears to have an oddity that was once yours, but that you lost in a game of chance years ago.

Additional Equipment: You have a crystal lens. When you shine light through it, the light extends for double the normal distance.

Radiant Esoteries: If you perform esoteries, those that would normally use force or other energy instead use light and heat. For example, when you use Ward, light dapples your body and flares when you would be attacked, preventing your enemies from landing a solid blow.

Minor Effect Suggestions: A flash of light leaves the creature dazzled. The difficulty of defense actions to resist the creature's attacks decreases by one step.

Major Effect Suggestions: An intense flash of light leaves the creature blinded for one minute.

Tier 1: Enlightened. You are trained in any perception task that involves sight. Enabler.

Illuminating Touch (1 Intellect point). You touch an object, and that object sheds light to illuminate everything in short range. The light remains until you use an action to touch the object again. Action.

Tier 2: Dazzling Radiance (2 Intellect points). You send a barrage of dazzling colors at a creature within short range. This attack is an Intellect action, and, if successful, it deals 2 points of damage to the target. In addition, until the end of the next round, the difficulty of all defense actions to resist the target's attacks is reduced by one step. The difficulty is not reduced if the target relies on senses other than sight to "see." Action.

Tier 3: Burning Light (3 Intellect points). You send a beam of light at a creature within long range and then tighten the beam until it burns. This attack is an Intellect action. If successful, it deals 5 points of damage to the target. Action.

Tier 4: Sunlight (3 Intellect points). A mote of light travels from you to a spot you choose within 100 feet (30 m). When the mote reaches that spot, it flares and casts bright light in a 200-foot (61 m) radius, and darkness within 1,000 feet (305 m) of the light becomes dim light. The light lasts for one hour or until you use an action to dismiss it. Action.

Tier 5: Disappear (4 Intellect points). You bend light that falls on you so you seem to disappear. You are invisible to other creatures for ten minutes. While invisible, you are specialized in stealth and Speed defense tasks. This effect ends if you do something to reveal your presence or position—attacking, performing an esotery, using an ability, moving a large object, and so on. If this occurs, you can regain the remaining invisibility effect by taking an action to focus on hiding your position. Action to initiate or reinitiate.

Tier 6: Living Light (5 Intellect points). Your body dissolves into a cloud of photons that instantly travel to a location you choose and then reform. You can choose any open space big enough to contain you that you can see within long range. You disappear and almost instantly reappear in the space you chose. It takes until the end of the round for your body to become fully solid, so until the start of the next round, you take half damage (minimum 1 point) from all physical sources. Action.

REFORGES COMPLETELY

Only varjellen characters can use this focus.

Varjellens can reconfigure their internal structures in a process they call reforging. The rare varjellen somamancer is one that learns to take this process much farther, reshaping its entire musculature, skeleton, and internal systems for great advantage. It isn't pretty, and it isn't easy, but it's worth it.

Whatever you wear is probably loose, easy to clean, and easy to put on and take off. After all, when you need to reassemble your internal organs, you don't want to worry about changing your clothes.

Connection: Choose one of the following.

1. Pick one other non-varjellen PC. You never seem to understand that character's moods or emotions.

2. Pick one other PC. He seems unduly interested in your skills. It's up to him whether he is fascinated or disturbed by them.

3. Pick two other non-varjellen PCs. These characters have said unkind things about varjellens when they thought you couldn't hear.

4. Pick one other non-varjellen PC. She seems to understand varjellens better than any non-varjellen you've ever known.

Minor Effect Suggestions: You restore 2 points to one of your stat Pools.

Major Effect Suggestions: The difficulty of your next action is decreased by two steps.

Tier 1: Rapid Reforging. Your reforging can be completed in an action, not an hour. Action.

Suitability: You have 3 additional points to permanently distribute among your stat Pools, as you wish. Enabler.

Tier 2: Elasticity (2 Might points). You rework your musculature and bone structure so that your arms or legs (or both) are about twice as long for ten minutes. Action to initiate.

Toughness (2 Might points). You rework your flesh and bones so that they are hardier and can resist damage more effectively. You gain +2 to Armor for ten minutes. Action to initiate.

Tier 3: Reconfigure (3 Might points). You gain +1 to your Speed Edge or your Might Edge (your choice) for 28 hours. Action to initiate.

Tier 4: Built for Speed (4 Might points). You reconfigure your shape so that you can move much faster. You can move a short distance as part of another action, you can move a long distance as an action, or—if you succeed at a Speed-based task—you can move 200 feet (61 m) as an action. This effect lasts for 28 hours. Action to initiate.

Tier 5: Efficient Shape (6 Might points). You can reconfigure your muscles and skeletal structure to gain an asset in a physical task of your choosing (such as climbing, swimming, running, and so on) for one hour. This includes melee or ranged attacks. Action to initiate.

Tier 6: Health and Vigor. You finally learn to give your body its optimal configuration. You are trained in Might defense tasks, and you gain 3 additional points to add to each of your stat Pools. You always roll the maximum when you make a recovery roll.

Reforges Completely GM Intrusions: *Internal self-surgery is more of an art than a science, and sometimes things don't go quite as planned. Recent reforgings can have weak spots, causing muscles to lock up temporarily or lungs to need more air than they're actually getting.*

SEES BEYOND

Unlike most people, you know there are far more than three dimensions. More colors than can be found in the rainbow. More things in the world than most can see, sense, or even understand. With practice and help (through drugs, lenses, manipulated energy fields, or a combination of all three), you can perceive things that others cannot.

What you see in other dimensions has changed your understanding of even the most basic things like weapon and dress. Where others might see your drab outfit and plain weapons, you see something entirely different—myriad colors and patterns that showcase your unique vision of the world. Your weapons likely bear marks of other dimensions as well.

Connection: Choose one of the following.

1. Pick one other PC. You are fairly certain that this character doesn't believe that your abilities are real.

2. Pick one other PC. You see a gathering of energy and colors on this character that seem to imply that she too can see beyond. Whether you ask her about it is up to you.

3. Pick one other PC. Whenever this character is near, your abilities seem to take longer and become more difficult.

4. Pick one other PC. Wherever this character goes, you are aware of the general distance and direction of his location.

Additional Equipment: You have a single item of your choosing—drugs, lenses, or a piece of the numenera—that helps you perceive things that others cannot.

Minor Effect Suggestions: The period of concentration needed is cut in half.

Major Effect Suggestions: You see even more than you normally do and can ask the GM one question about what you're looking at.

Tier 1: See the Unseen. You can perceive creatures and objects that are normally invisible, out of phase, or only partially in this universe. When looking for things more conventionally hidden, the difficulty of the task is also reduced by one step. Enabler.

Tier 2: See Through Matter (3 Intellect points). You can see through matter as if it were transparent (or you had "x-ray vision"). You can see through up to 6 inches (15 cm) of material for one round, although some materials might be harder to see through than others. Action.

Tier 3: Find the Hidden (4+ Intellect points). You see the traceries of objects as they move through space and time. You can sense the distance and direction of any specific inanimate object that you once touched. This takes anywhere from one action to hours of concentration, depending on what the GM feels is appropriate due to time, distance, or other mitigating circumstances. However, you don't know in advance how long it will take. If you use at least two levels of Effort, once you have established the distance and direction, you remain in contact with the object for one hour per level of Effort used. Thus, if it moves, you are aware of its new position. Action to initiate; action each round to concentrate.

Tier 4: Remote Viewing (6 Intellect points). Distance is an illusion, as all space is one space. With great concentration, you can see another place. This ability can be used in one of two different ways:

• Distance and direction. Pick a spot a specific distance away and in a specific direction. For one minute, you see from that vantage point, as if that was where you stood.

• Think of a place that you have seen before, either conventionally or using the other application of this power. For one minute, you see from that vantage point, as if that was where you stood.

Either application takes anywhere from one action to hours of concentration, depending on what the GM feels is appropriate due to time, distance, or other mitigating circumstances. However, you don't know in advance how long it will take. Action to initiate; action each round to concentrate.

Tier 5: See Through Time (7 Intellect points). Time is an illusion, as all time is one time. With great concentration, you can see into another time. You specify a time period regarding the place where you now stand. Interestingly, the easiest time to view is about one hundred years in the past or future (difficulty 5). Viewing farther back or ahead grows more difficult, so that a million years in the past or future, or moments behind or ahead of the present, are both difficulty 10.

This takes anywhere from one action to hours of concentration, depending on what the GM feels is appropriate due to time, distance, or other mitigating circumstances. However, you don't know in advance how long it will take. Action to initiate; action each round to concentrate.

Tier 6: Total Awareness. You possess such a high level of awareness that it's very difficult to surprise, hide, or sneak up on you. The difficulty of any initiative or perception task that you attempt is reduced by three steps. Enabler.

SEPARATES MIND FROM BODY

Your mind is to your body as a captain is to her ship. Your body obeys your commands, moving and behaving as you direct it, but at any time you choose, your mind can wriggle free from its container and explore the world freely. When you project your mind, there are few places you cannot go, few secrets that can remain hidden from you.

You probably regard your body as merely a vessel. As a result, you're not likely to put a lot of effort in style or keeping yourself especially clean. Your clothing is likely tattered and dirty.

Nanos are the ones mostly likely to learn the art of projection. Jacks, however, find projection useful as it expands their options for snooping around without drawing attention.

Connection: Choose one of the following.

1. Pick one other PC. Through a quirk of fate or careful cultivation (your choice), you always know where that character is in relation to you. You are always aware of the direction and distance you must travel to reach him.

2. Pick two other PCs. You believe that while using your Third Eye power, you once saw them engaged in something covert and possibly illegal. It's up to those characters whether one, both, or neither were actually involved.

3. Pick one other PC. For reasons beyond understanding, your focus abilities do not function when she is next to you and in your field of vision.

4. Pick one other PC. He is fascinated by your skills and wants to study you more closely. It's up to you whether or not you let him.

Additional Equipment: You possess an oddity that looks like a silvery ball, about 3 inches (7.6 cm) in diameter. The ball's highly polished surface looks as if it reflects your surroundings, but examining its surface reveals it reflects the surroundings of another location, one you have not yet found. In the images shown on the ball, you have seen many strange and unsettling things.

Mental Esoteries: If you have the Mind Reading or Sensor esotery, you're

automatically trained in it. If you have both, you're trained in both. Enabler.

Minor Effect Suggestions: You have an asset on any action that involves using your senses, such as perceiving or attacking, until the end of the next round.

Major Effect Suggestions: Your Intellect Edge increases by 1 until the end of the next round.

Tier 1: Third Eye (1 Intellect point). You visualize a place within short range and cast your mind to that place, creating an immobile, invisible sensor for one minute or until you choose to end this ability. While using your third eye, you see through your sensor instead of your eyes using your normal visual abilities. You may perceive the area around your body using your other senses as normal. Action.

Separates Mind From Body GM Intrusions: Reuniting mind and body can sometimes be disorienting and require a character to spend a few moments to get his or her bearings.

Mind Reading, page 37
Sensor, page 37

Tier 2: Open Mind (3 Intellect points). You open your mind to increase your awareness. The difficulty of any task involving perception is decreased by one step. While you have this asset and you are conscious and able to take actions, other characters gain no benefit for surprising you. The effect lasts for one hour. Action.

   Sharp Senses. You are trained in all tasks involving perception. Enabler.

Tier 3: Roaming Third Eye (3 Intellect points). When you use your Third Eye ability, you can place the sensor anywhere within long range. In addition, until that ability ends, you can use an action to move the sensor anywhere within short range of its starting position. Enabler.

Tier 4: Sensor. You gain the Sensor esotery. If you already have this esotery, you may choose another esotery from the nano's third tier or lower. Enabler.

   Improved Sensor (2 Intellect points). When you use Sensor, you can place the sensor anywhere you choose within long range. Enabler.

Tier 5: Psychic Passenger (6 Intellect points). You place your mind into the body of a willing creature you choose within short range and remain in that body for up to one hour. Your own body falls down and becomes insensate until this ability ends.

   You see, hear, smell, touch, and taste using the senses of the character whose body you inhabit. When you speak, the words come from your defenseless body, and the character you inhabit hears those words in his mind.

   The character you inhabit can use your Intellect Edge in place of his own. In addition, you and the character have an asset on any task that involves perception.

   When you take an action, you use the character's body to perform that action if he allows it. Action to initiate.

Tier 6: Mental Projection (6+ Intellect points). Your mind fully leaves your body and manifests anywhere you choose within immediate range. Your projected mind can remain apart from your body for up to 28 hours. This effect ends early if your Intellect Pool is reduced to 0 or if your projection touches your resting body.

   Your disembodied mind has a form that looks just like you. It has little physical substance, however, and its frayed edges trail off into nothingness. You control this body as if it were your normal body and can act and move

as you normally would with a few exceptions.

   You can move through solid objects as if they weren't there, and you ignore any terrain feature that would impede your movement.

   Your attacks deal half damage, and you take half damage from physical sources. Regardless of the source, however, you take all damage as Intellect damage.

   Your mind can travel up to 1 mile (1.6 km) from your body. Instead of applying Effort to decrease the difficulty, you can extend the range that you can travel by 1 mile for each level of Effort you apply.

   Your physical body is helpless until this effect ends. You cannot use your senses to perceive anything. For example, your body could sustain a significant injury, and you wouldn't know it. Your body cannot take Intellect damage, so if your body takes enough damage to reduce both your Might Pool and your Speed Pool to 0, your mind snaps back to your body, and you are stunned until the end of the next round as you try to reorient yourself to your predicament. Action to initiate.

SIPHONS POWER

You are an energy vampire, draining power from machines or living creatures. You use this power to restore your own physical energy reserves. Perhaps you take great joy in this ability, or perhaps you grudgingly accept it as a boon to yourself and your companions and use it only when you must. Either way, you are likely feared and unwelcome in many communities for your dangerous powers. You might try to conceal your true nature, dressing so that you don't attract attention and give yourself away, or perhaps you flaunt it, using the rumors to your advantage, wearing black clothing and embodying a sinister countenance.

   Although most people assume that energy vampires are usually nanos, glaives and jacks can benefit as much or more from the ability to siphon energy for their physical bodies.

   Connection: Choose one of the following.

   1. Pick one other PC. This character is immune to your powers for some inexplicable reason.

   2. Pick one other PC. This character appears to think of you as some kind of monster.

   3. Pick one other PC with a living or machine companion. This character seems convinced that you're going to use his companion for your own ill-gotten purposes.

   4. Pick one other PC. You believe she can help you control and understand your abilities, if you can get her to talk about it.

Siphons Power GM Intrusions: Sometimes power drained from another source carries with it something unwanted— compulsions, afflictions, or alien thoughts. Siphoned power can overload the character, causing feedback.

Minor Effect Suggestions: When draining, you gain 2 additional points to divide among your Speed Pool and Might Pool.

Major Effect Suggestions: When draining, you gain 5 additional points to divide among your Speed Pool and Might Pool.

Tier 1: Drain Machine (2 Intellect points). You can drain the power from an artifact or device you touch, allowing you to regain 1 point per level of the device. You can use this point to restore your Might Pool or Speed Pool. You regain points at the rate of 1 point per minute and must give your full concentration to the process during this time. The GM determines whether the device is fully drained (likely true of most handheld or smaller devices) or retains some power (likely true of large machines). Action to initiate.

Tier 2: Drain Creature (2 Intellect points). You can drain the power from a living creature you touch, allowing you to regain 1 point per level of the creature. You can use this point to restore your Might Pool or Speed Pool. You regain points at the rate of 1 point per minute and must give your full concentration to the process during this time, meaning that the creature probably has to be subdued in some fashion, because it loses 3 points of health for every point you gain. Creatures drained of all their health die. (PCs drained lose points from their Pools.) Action to initiate.

Tier 3: Quick Drain (3 Intellect points). You can drain the power from a machine or a living creature you touch, allowing you to regain up to 3 points to restore your Might Pool or Speed Pool. You regain the points immediately. If the device is level 3 or lower, it is fully drained. Otherwise, the GM decides what happens to it. Creatures drained suffer 5 points of damage. After using Quick Drain on a device or creature, you can't drain it again using any of your abilities. Action.

Tier 4: Drain at a Distance. You can use your Drain Machine, Drain Creature, or Quick Drain abilities on any target within short range. Enabler.

Tier 5: Share the Power. You can take points that you have gained through draining and give them to another creature that you touch. PC recipients can distribute the points to any of their stat Pools, while NPC recipients restore lost health. Action.

Automatons and other living machines should be treated as creatures, not machines, for the purposes of siphoning power from them.

Tier 6: Consume (6 Intellect points). You can drain the power from a machine or a living creature you touch, allowing you to regain up to 7 points to restore your Might Pool or Speed Pool. You regain the points immediately. If the device is level 5 or lower, it is entirely consumed and disappears. Otherwise, the GM decides what happens to it. Creatures drained suffer 10 points of damage. If that is enough to kill them, they are entirely consumed and disappear. After using Consume on a device or creature, you can't drain it again using any of your abilities. Action.

STANDS LIKE A BASTION

You are a wall. A stone. An island against a storm of weapons and words. Nothing moves you. Nothing even really dents you. Perhaps it's your physical size that lends you such stopping power, perhaps you've enhanced your physique with mechanisms and machinery, or perhaps it's merely your incredible strength of will that forces foes to stay their swings.

Your armor is probably just like you: solid,

Stands Like a Bastion GM Intrusions: *Armor that you rely on falls apart. A weakness in your body causes ripple effects. Small foes conspire against you in ways you don't expect.*

strong, and utterly impenetrable. Every flourish and bit of flair—if you have any—does double duty as protection.

Glaives are often suited for this focus, but well-armored jacks can sometimes step into this role.

Connection: Choose one of the following.

1. Pick one other PC. You feel indebted to this character and go out of your way to protect her from harm.

2. Pick one other PC. You once saved this character from a dangerous situation.

3. Pick one other PC. This character once ran full bore into you while running away from... something. You stopped him just by being in the wrong place at the wrong time, but he seems to hold it against you.

4. Pick two other PCs. You would like to ask them to help you train by attacking you at the same time, but you're uncertain how to approach them with this request.

Additional Equipment: You have armor of your choice and a shield.

Minor Effect Suggestions: You add +2 to Armor.

Major Effect Suggestions: You regain 2 points to your Might Pool.

Tier 1: Experienced Defender. If you wear armor of any kind, you gain +1 to Armor.

Practiced in Armor. You can wear armor for long periods of time without tiring and can compensate for slowed reactions from wearing armor. You can wear any kind of armor. You reduce the Might cost per hour for wearing armor and the Speed Pool reduction for wearing armor by 2. Enabler.

Tier 2: Resist the Elements. You resist heat, cold, and similar extremes. You have a special +2 bonus to Armor against ambient damage or other damage that would normally ignore Armor.

Tier 3: Unmovable (3 Might points). You avoid being knocked down, pushed back, or moved against your will as long as you are upright and able to take actions. Enabler.

Mighty. You gain 5 additional points to your Might Pool. Enabler.

Tier 4: Living Wall (3 Might points). You specify a confined area—such as an open doorway, a hallway, or a space between two trees—where you stand. For the next ten minutes, if anyone attempts to enter or pass through that area and you don't wish it, you make an automatic attack against them. If you

hit, not only do you inflict damage, but they must also stop their movement. Enabler.

Tier 5: Hardiness. You are trained in Might defense tasks.

Mastery With Armor. When you wear any armor, you reduce the armor's penalties (Might cost and Speed reduction) to 0. Enabler.

Tier 6: Shield Training. If you use a shield, the difficulty of Speed defense tasks is decreased by two steps instead of one. Enabler.

Wall With Teeth: You inflict 2 additional points of damage with all attacks when using your Living Wall ability.

THROWS WITH DEADLY ACCURACY

Sometimes you wonder if your hand and your mind's eye are connected in an intricate perfection of timing and aim. Everything that leaves your hand goes exactly where you'd like it to and at the range and speed to make the perfect impact. Your expertise might be in carefully hewn throwing daggers and sisks, or perhaps you use whatever's nearby.

What you wear doesn't matter, as long as it doesn't come between you and your throwing implement. Lots of pockets, equipment belts, and pouches make it easy to keep your preferred weapons close at hand. You might even have a hat with a variety of throwing items tucked into its brim, ready to meet their target with your perfect aim.

Connection: Choose one of the following.

1. Pick one other PC. You believe that this character shows potential for being an excellent ranged attacker, but you don't know if she would be interested in the rigorous training and practice required.

2. Pick one other PC. This character once saved you from a dangerous situation.

3. Pick one other PC. You owe this character 10 shins.

4. Pick one other PC. He is always getting in the way. If the GM determines that your attack strikes the wrong target, it almost always hits this character.

Additional Equipment: You have three throwing weapons of your choice.

Minor Effect Suggestions: You hit your target in the eye and blind him for one round.

Major Effect Suggestions: You strike your target in a limb, making that limb useless for the next minute.

Throws With Deadly Accuracy GM Intrusions: Missed attacks strike the wrong target. Ricochets can be dangerous. Improvised weapons break.

Glaives who Stand LIke a Bastian already have Practiced in Armor. They can choose an additional Tier 1 fighting move instead.

Tier 1: Precision. You deal 2 additional points of damage with attacks using weapons that you throw. Enabler.

Tier 2: Careful Aim. You are trained in attacks with all weapons that you throw. Enabler.

Tier 3: Rapid Fire (2 Speed points). When you make an attack by throwing a light weapon, you can draw another light weapon and make another thrown attack against the same target or a different target as part of the same action. Action.

Tier 4: Everything Is a Weapon. You can take any small object—a shin, a pen, a bottle, a stone, and so on—and throw it with such force and precision that it inflicts damage as a light weapon. Enabler.

    Deadly Aim. You are specialized in attacks with all weapons that you throw. Enabler.

Tier 5: Spray Attack (5 Speed points). With a large handful of small objects—tiny knives, shuriken, stones, jagged bits of metal, shins, or whatever is on hand—you attack every creature in an immediate area within short range. You must make attack rolls against each target. The difficulty of each attack is increased by one step. You inflict 3 points of damage on targets you hit. Action.

Tier 6: Force and Accuracy: You inflict 3 additional points of damage with attacks using weapons that you throw. Enabler.

TRAVELS THROUGH TIME

You have the unusual ability to travel through time in a way others can never dream of. You have likely experienced jumps where time seems to have passed but you have no memory of what happened. You probably also suffer from déjà vu, sensing that you have been in a situation or witnessed an event before and are now experiencing it all over again. You have begun to realize the extent of your powers and work to master them so that perhaps one day you can travel farther into the future or deeper into the past.

Time travel poses many risks. Often, you have no clear sense about what the future might hold or what might have been happening in the spot where you appear when you travel to the past. Death waits for the bold and the incautious.

Worse than mishap, you must guard against paradox. When you change an event in the past, you could inadvertently cause the future to be rewritten. On the other hand, cosmic forces may move in to correct paradoxes by changing circumstances to accommodate the revision, causing your memories to become false ones when the world you know changes to adapt to your meddling. Of course, if you attempt anything too radical, the universe might write you out of existence so that your efforts to change the past never occur.

You likely wear clothing and have personal effects in a range of styles, choosing items from many different periods. This eclectic approach to your possessions may give you a shabby appearance or make you look strange and alien to others in the present.

Any type of character can have this focus, though its power is extraordinarily rare.

Connection: Choose one of the following.

1. Pick one other PC. You are either a distant ancestor or a descendant of that character. He served as a focal point for your travel and anchors you to the present.

2. Pick one other PC. For some reason, when you use your Anticipation power to look ahead, you specifically see how her future might unfold. You can choose whether or not to tell her what you see.

3. Pick one other PC. You secretly believe that he can also travel through time, since you once fought a person who looked exactly like him.

4. Pick one other PC. You once stepped forward in time to save her from death, but she doesn't know it. You may choose whether or not to tell her.

Additional Equipment: You have two additional oddities.

Temporal Esoteries: If you perform esoteries, time appears to slow down when you use them. You and everything around you moves in slow motion for a moment, and then time snaps back into place. The temporal distortion changes nothing about the effects of your esoteries except for the appearance of the world around you.

Minor Effect Suggestions: One creature you choose within short range either acts first or acts last during the next round.

Major Effect Suggestions: You step a few moments into the future. To other characters, it looks as if you disappeared. At the start of the next round, you reappear and you have an asset for any task you perform during that round.

Travels Through Time GM Intrusions: *Moving through time creates countless possibilities for paradoxes to occur, both small and large. As reality flows in to correct these snarls in time, certain events the character experienced may become rewritten. Other people might remember events differently than the time traveler does.*

FOR THE GM: MANAGING TIME TRAVEL

Although time travel offers plenty of grist for the storytelling mill, it also brings plenty of complications. If a player chooses this focus and you allow it, you need to decide whether the character can change history by traveling through time.

The easiest way to manage time travel is to simply say that the characters jump to a different timeline when they move forward or backward through time. Anything they do while displaced in time affects only events on that line.

The point the PCs left becomes a nexus of many timelines. Characters returning to that point might find themselves in their original time, in which case nothing they altered in the past affects their present or future, or they might be in a different timeline, where their past actions have had a great effect on the current world.

The biggest benefit of the multiple timelines approach is that it sidesteps the problems of paradoxes. Whenever a paradox would occur, the characters create another timeline instead. So if a PC goes back in time to a point before he is born and kills his grandfather, he erases himself from that timeline, but not from his own. Thus, the character would continue to exist.

You can use other methods for managing time travel, allowing characters to change past events to create a new future, paradoxes be damned. Or you might have the PCs merely observe, unable to interact with anything outside of the point you decide is the present.

Tier 1: Anticipation (1 Intellect point). You look ahead to see how your actions might unfold. You have an asset for the first task you perform before the end of the next round. Enabler.

Tier 2: See History (4 Intellect points). You touch an object and immediately visualize up to three significant events that involved the object or happened near it at some point in the past, starting with the most recent. The events are those that involve intense emotion or sensation, or that had an impact on the way history unfolded after the event. The GM decides whether you see the event, gain some understanding of what happened, or receive impressions of what was experienced. Afterward, you have an asset on any task to identify the object. Action.

Tier 3: Temporal Acceleration (5 Intellect points). You or one willing character you touch moves more quickly through time. The effect lasts for one minute. Everything moves more slowly for the affected character, while to all others, the character seems to move at preternatural speed. The character has an asset on all tasks until the effect ends. After the effect ends, the difficulty of all tasks is increased by one step for one hour because the character is exhausted and disoriented by the experience. Action to initiate.

Tier 4: Temporal Dislocation (7 Intellect points). You disappear and travel up to one hour into the future or the past. You remain there until you catch up to the present or the present catches up to you. While dislocated in time, you perceive events as they transpire from your position using your normal senses.

No other character can see you or interact with you. Similarly, you cannot interact with your environment. Action to initiate.

Tier 5: Time Loop (7 Intellect points). You call yourself from a few moments in the future to help you in the present. Your future self appears anywhere you choose within immediate range and remains until the end of the next round, at which point both you and your future self disappear. At the end of the next round, you reappear in the space your future self left when he disappeared.

Your future self shares your stats, so any damage that either of you takes applies to the same stat Pools. When you appear from the future, you may immediately use an action. During the next round, your present self and your future self both act.

If an attack against your future self deals damage sufficient to kill you, your future self dies, but you don't die until after the effect causes you to disappear. Action to initiate.

Tier 6: Time Travel (10+ Intellect points). You and up to three willing characters you choose within immediate range travel to a point in time that you specify when you use this ability. The point in time must be within ten years of the present. For each level of Effort applied, you can travel ten more years. When you appear in the new moment in time, you do so in the same position you were in when you used this ability. Upon arriving at your temporal destination, you and each character that traveled with you are stunned for one minute. In order to return to the original time, you must use the power again. Action.

OPTIONAL AND ADDITIONAL RULES

This final chapter offers a number of different options for Numenera players and GMs. You can use these, modify them, or simply look upon them as ideas and guidelines for your own game.

CUSTOMIZING CHARACTERS

Character creation in Numenera is meant to be simple and fast. However, it's also meant to provide players with the character they want to play. Sometimes, a player wants more than the options provided, even when you add in all the new options this book offers. For these players, some tweaking and modifying is required.

The Numenera corebook already provides guidelines for modifying or creating your own new types, descriptors, and foci. Read through those optional rules before using the guidelines here.

SKILLS FROM BACKGROUNDS

A glaive's background says that he worked in a smithy as a young lad. But there's no way a glaive can begin with weaponsmithing as a skill (he can get this skill as he progresses). Shouldn't he start with that skill? This question has four potential answers.

1. *No.* He might know the basics of the task. However, a skill doesn't represent a simple familiarity, but extensive training, experience, or talent. Not everyone who works in a restaurant is a chef.

2. *Sure.* In the scope of things, will weaponsmithing wreck the game or make the character unplayable? Is it unfair to the other players? Probably not. For that matter, give all the characters a background skill. Require that it ties into the character's actual background and doesn't have a lot of direct adventuring applications. For example, a PC can have cooking, animal care, philosophy, or woodworking, but not climbing, sneaking, or anything similar, and certainly not a skill with attack or defense.

3. *Yes.* Use the Experience Point Advance optional rules, where the character takes on a story complication in exchange for receiving 4 XP to buy the new skill.

4. *Yes.* Allow the player to have an XP deficit. The character starts with the desired skill, but

Customizing Character Types, page 117

Customizing Descriptors, page 117

Customizing Foci, page 118

XP Advance, page 119

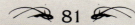

Characters should always be customized in the name of their concept, background, and story, and never simply to make a better "character build." These guidelines should never be used for min-maxing to get a more powerful character.

Optional abilities can be purchased instead of taking a standard character benefit, page 24

before he can gain any of the four benefits required to advance to the next tier, the player must pay off this deficit. It's probably unwise to allow a character to start with a deficit of greater than 4 XP.

TRADING ABILITIES

Sometimes a player wants to be a nano but also wants to wear armor without a penalty. To make armor easier to wear, you can use the rule that allows a character to purchase an ability other than one of the four benefits (usually a new skill).

But there are other options as well. On a case-by-case basis, you can take an ability from one type (or focus) and make it available to another type at the same tier (or perhaps a higher tier). This option should be used very conservatively, particularly since one of the main draws of a jack character is that jacks have access to abilities from both of the other types.

Moves Like a Cat, page 68
Quick Strike, page 68

If you want a slightly more "balanced" alternative, require that the character sacrifice something to gain something. If a nano wants a glaive ability, she has to give up some aspect of being a nano. Perhaps she can wear armor with the Practiced in Armor ability, but she has to give up her numenera knowledge, or she can use cyphers only like a glaive, and so on.

This works best for nonvariable abilities. But what about other tier abilities? Sometimes, a player might want just one ability from another type. For example, a glaive wants to use a particular trick of the trade as a fighting move. That's probably okay, but again, it should be done on a case-by-case basis and very rarely. And it's still viable to ask that player to give something up. For example, if a glaive wants a trick of the trade at second tier, he should give up one of the second-tier fighting move options permanently.

Bears a Halo of Fire, page 52
Carries a Quiver, page 54

What do you do in the opposite situation, where a player has a nonvariable ability that he doesn't want? In most cases, the answer probably is: do nothing. Just because a glaive doesn't want to wear armor, that doesn't

mean her Practiced in Armor ability is a waste. She might need it later on. But in some cases, that nonvariable ability can be swapped for something else—almost always something of less "value." In the case of the no-armor glaive, perhaps she gets training in a relatively innocuous skill. For higher-tier abilities, the trade is for a lower-tier ability.

MODIFYING ABILITIES

Characters can spend additional points or make a special roll to make an ability work beyond the bounds of its normal parameters. This is called modifying an ability, and it works on the fly.

But what if a player wants to modify an ability permanently? What if a character who Moves Like a Cat wants her fourth-tier Quick Strike ability to stun foes rather than daze them? Consider the following questions.

Is the modified ability more powerful?
In our example, it is, because stunned foes lose their next action, while dazed foes simply take a penalty to actions. If the answer is yes, a permanent price must be paid for the modification. First of all, increase the point cost (if any) by at least 50 percent.

Alternatively, require that a level of Effort be used with the ability. If there is no cost—if the ability is always active, for example—give it a duration (perhaps an hour) and a point cost. Usually the point cost would be the tier + 1.

Is the modified ability less powerful?
If so, reduce the point cost by at least 50 percent. If the ability has no cost to reduce, consider giving the character an extra skill.

Is the modified ability about the same?
Then call it even.

Sometimes a player wants to have an entirely new ability—not one from another type or focus, and not just a modification of an existing ability. In this case, the player and

the GM should work out the details together, basing the power level of the new ability on the one that it is replacing. This is tricky, of course, but the broad strokes—damage inflicted, point cost, and so on—can be transferred if applicable, and minor aspects like range and duration should just fit the new ability rather than be a "balance" consideration.

ADDITIONAL CONNECTIONS

The foci in this book have four connection options rather than the one option given for the foci in the Numenera corebook. The additional options add more flexibility and replayability to the game.

If you like this idea and want to use it with the foci in the corebook, this section presents four connection options for each focus.

BEARS A HALO OF FIRE

1. Pick one other PC. Through a quirk of fate, your fire cannot harm that character.

2. Pick one other PC. You recently discovered that if she stands near you when you use your Shroud of Flame ability, she too becomes covered in flames. This doesn't harm her, and anyone who tries to touch her or strike her with a melee attack suffers 1 point of damage. She must remain within short range of you.

3. Pick one other PC. He had a devastating experience with fire in his past and must decide how to react to your constant use of flame around him.

4. Pick one other PC. For some reason, one of his limbs is especially vulnerable to your flames. Occasionally when you use Hurl Flame to harm a foe, his vulnerable body part bursts into flame. The flame doesn't harm him or his equipment, but it can be an impediment during combat due to surprise.

CARRIES A QUIVER

1. Pick one other PC to be the true friend who gave you the excellent bow that you currently use. Secretly pick a second PC (preferably one who is likely to get in the way of your attacks). When you miss with a bow and the GM rules that you struck someone other than your target, you hit the second character, if possible.

2. Pick one other PC that you've known for a while. The two of you used to do an act where you shot an apple out of her mouth, either for money or just the enjoyment of friends. One time you missed and hit her in the cheek. She may or may not still bear a physical or mental scar from this experience. Either way, you never did your act again.

3. Pick one other PC who is interested in studying archery. He is a quick learner, and if you spend one hour teaching him a few of your secrets, you both gain +1 to any die rolls when you fight the same foe using your bows.

4. Pick one other PC. That person brings up strong emotions in you, whether of anger, desire, or something else. If she is within short range while you're using your bow, you find it difficult to concentrate and shoot straight.

COMMANDS MENTAL POWERS

1. Pick one other PC. You have found that this character is particularly tuned into your mental powers. While you're within short range of him, the two of you are always in telepathic contact, and he is never harmed by your Psychic Burst.

2. Pick one other PC. She is what you might call a "loud thinker," and her thoughts sometimes come through to you when you are within short range, even when you're not using your Mind Reading ability. You can't seem to turn this off. Whether your tell her or not is up to you.

3. Pick one other PC. For some reason, he seems to act as an antenna for your mental powers. If the two of you are touching, your Telepathic and Mind Reading abilities sometimes extend to long range.

4. Pick one other PC. Your close mentor or teacher once used Mind Control on her and forced her to do something against her will. To this day, you haven't talked about it, but you are both intensely aware of the connection.

CONTROLS BEASTS

1. Pick one other PC. That character seems to disturb your creatures in a way that you can't explain. You know that you must keep your animals away from him if possible, or you might lose control of them.

2. Pick one other PC. The creature that you're bonded with seems to have a special bond with this other person as well. You must decide whether it brings up feelings of jealousy or camaraderie within you and

whether to thwart the connection or help it blossom.

3. Pick one other PC. Recently, he accidentally (or perhaps intentionally) put your beast companion in a position of danger. Your companion is now nervous around him, and you are struggling with your own emotional response to the incident.

4. Pick one other PC. She dislikes beasts of all kinds, seeing them as little more than food or prey. You hope that exposing her to your beast companion will change her mind. It's up to that player how her character responds to the experience.

CONTROLS GRAVITY

1. Pick one other PC. In the recent past, while using your gravitational powers, you accidentally sent that character hurtling into the air or plummeting toward the ground. Either way, she barely survived. It is up to the player of that character to decide whether she resents, fears, or forgives you.

2. Pick one other PC whose focus intertwines with yours. This odd connection affects her in some way. For example, if the character Carries a Quiver, then your ability to manipulate gravity sometimes extends the range of her arrows. If she Entertains, her jumps, dances, and juggling balls seem less bound by the laws of gravity. If she Masters Weaponry, her weapons sometimes feel lighter.

3. Pick one other PC. He is deathly afraid of heights. Through your ability to control gravity, you would like to teach him how to be more comfortable with his feet off the ground. He must decide whether or not to take you up on your offer.

4. Pick one other PC. She is skeptical of your ability to control gravity and thinks it's just one big illusion. She might even attempt to discredit you or discover the "secret" behind your so-called skills.

CRAFTS ILLUSIONS

1. Pick one other PC. This character is never fooled by your illusions and is never affected by the trickery of your special abilities. You can choose whether or not you know this fact.

2. Pick one other PC. He has a special angle on your illusions and can sometimes point out potential places of weakness.

3. Pick two other PCs who are willing to be trained as your assistants. When you use your Minor Illusion ability, if both of these characters are in immediate range, they can

It's tempting to choose the connection that makes your character more powerful somehow, but in truth it's sometimes the ones that seem more like a drawback that lead to fun and interesting situations in your game.

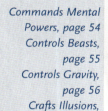

assist you, together decreasing the difficulty of your action by one step.

4. Pick one other PC. That character's face is so intriguing to you in a way you don't understand that your minor illusions sometimes look like him, even when you don't intend them to.

CRAFTS UNIQUE OBJECTS

1. Pick one other PC. The character has an extra item of regular equipment that you fashioned for her. (She chooses the item.)

2. Pick one other PC. She seems to have in her possession an object that you made for someone else a long time ago.

3. Pick one other PC. He has commissioned you to create something for him. You've already been paid but haven't yet completed the item.

4. Pick one PC. You've seen that character admiring your crafting skills many times. Perhaps he would like a lesson. (You won't know until you ask.)

EMPLOYS MAGNETISM

1. Pick one other PC. Whenever you use your powers, the metallic items on that character's body shudder, rattle, clink, and shake if he is within short range.

2. Pick one other PC. You worked together in the past, and the job ended badly.

3. Pick two other PCs. While practicing your Diamagnetism ability, you once accidentally sent them careening into each other. You've never been able to repeat it. Whether you tell them that you've been trying to replicate the strange effect is up to you.

4. Pick one other PC who has metallic elements in his body. You're afraid to use your magnetism abilities near him because you once had a bad experience involving Move Metal and a (probably former) friend's mechanical eyes.

ENTERTAINS

1. Pick one other PC. This character is your worst critic. Your abilities to help or inspire others don't function for her.

2. Pick one other PC. He seems to really enjoy your attempts to entertain, and this brings out the performer in you. It's up to that character whether his appreciation is real or if he is just being polite.

3. Pick one other PC. She is so inspired and put at ease by your stories or other forms of entertainment when you use Levity that she gains +2 to her recovery rolls (instead of +1).

4. Pick one other PC. This person knows the secret to one of your favorite forms of

Crafts Unique Objects, page 58

Employs Magnetism, page 59

Entertains, page 60

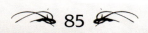

entertainment. You worry constantly that he will steal it or reveal it.

EXISTS PARTIALLY OUT OF PHASE

1. Pick one other PC. You have known that character for a while, and he helped you gain control of your phase states.

2. Pick one other PC. Sometime in his past, he had a devastating experience with going out of phase. Whether he chooses to tell you about it is up to him.

3. Pick one other PC. You once accidentally moved your hand right through her. It was clearly an unnerving experience for you both.

4. Pick two other PCs. They both really want to go out of phase and have been pestering you about it. But you're not convinced they even know what that phrase means.

EXPLORES DARK PLACES

1. Pick one other PC. This character has been your adventuring partner in previous expeditions, and the two of you work so well together that you both gain +1 to any die rolls when you collaborate on the same task, fight the same foe, and so on.

2. Pick two other PCs. You think you once saw them through a keyhole doing something illegal. You can choose whether or not to share that information. The characters can choose whether it was really them (it could have been neither, one, or both), and they may or may not share that information in return.

3. Pick one other PC. This person always seems to hear you, no matter how stealthy you try to be.

4. Pick one other PC. She is so loud in everything she does that you feel obligated to try to help her learn to move more quietly through the world. Whether or not she's interested is up to her.

FIGHTS WITH PANACHE

1. Pick one other PC. You're always trying to impress this character with your skill, wit, appearance, or bravado. Perhaps she is a rival, perhaps you need her respect, or perhaps you're romantically interested in her.

2. Pick one other PC. This character seems to anticipate your next move almost before you even begin it. When he collaborates with you on the same task or fights the same foe, you gain +1 to any die rolls.

3. Pick one other PC. You fear that she is jealous of your abilities and worry that it might lead to problems.

4. Pick one other PC. This character is so

enamored of your swashbuckling, entertaining ways during combat that he sometimes forgets to take action himself.

FOCUSES MIND OVER MATTER

1. Pick one other PC. This character can cause your telekinetic powers to act oddly. Every once in a while, if he stands directly next to you, your powers are cancelled, but at other times, they seem improved when used near him.

2. Pick one other PC. This person thinks that your powers are completely hypothetical.

3. Pick one other PC. You once joked that you could read her mind. Whether she found that exciting or utterly terrifying is up to her.

4. Pick one other PC. You feel strangely protective toward that character and plan to do your best to keep him from harm.

FUSES FLESH AND STEEL

1. Pick one other PC. This character knows your true nature, even if no one else does. If your components are not particularly hidden, she knows a different secret of yours, such as a preprogrammed word that will shut you down for ten minutes.

2. Pick one other PC. Being close to this person sometimes makes your mechanical parts vibrate slightly. You can decide whether this sensation is unnerving or pleasant.

3. Pick one other PC. You're pretty sure that he is just here to mine you for parts. He chooses whether or not this is true.

4. Pick one other PC who has mechanical parts. The two of you have bonded over conversations about this element you share, and you feel a special connection.

HOWLS AT THE MOON

1. Pick one other PC. That character is able to soothe you when you're in beast form. You'll never attack him while transformed, and if he spends three consecutive turns using his action to calm you down, you can revert to your normal form without having to make a roll.

2. Pick one other PC. You believe that he intends to convince you (or capture you) to join Ossam's Traveling Menagerie and Soaring Circus. He chooses whether or not this is true.

3. Pick two other PCs. They know that it's beneficial for you to kill and eat a creature while you're in beast form, and they often work together to make sure that happens.

4. Pick one other PC. Since she saw you

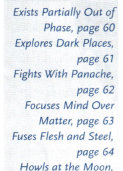

Ossam's Traveling Menagerie and Soaring Circus, page 165

in beast form, she has clearly been terrified of you. You are determined to show her that you're not as dangerous as she thinks.

HUNTS WITH GREAT SKILL

1. Pick one other PC. That person once saw you show surprising mercy toward your prey, and now you hope she keeps that information quiet—it might harm your reputation.

2. Pick one other PC. You accidentally caught her in one of your traps and she had to free herself.

3. Pick one other PC. Back in your bounty hunter days (which may or may not be over), you were hired to track down someone close to him.

4. Pick one other PC. You've noticed that it's almost impossible to track him, but you're determined to figure out a way.

LEADS

1. Pick one other PC. That character was once a follower of yours, but you have since grown to think of him as a peer.

2. Pick two other PCs. The three of you worked as a team on a mission long ago, but you had a falling out with both of them.

3. Pick one other PC. That person is an overly enthusiastic follower of yours. Whether you bask in the attention or find it overbearing is up to you.

4. Pick one other PC. You used to be in a relationship with that character, but it's long over.

LIVES IN THE WILDERNESS

1. Pick one other PC who isn't from the wilderness. You can't help but feel a little contempt for that character and her "civilized" ways, which show disdain for all things natural and (to your mind) true.

2. Pick one other PC. He is one of the few people that you are completely comfortable being around, and you are often surprised at how easily you let down your guard near him.

3. Pick one other PC. She once saved you from an uncomfortable social situation, and you still feel grateful.

4. Pick one other PC. This person seems to understand civilization in the same way that you understand the wilderness. You could choose to help each other or despise each other for this different way of seeing the world.

MASTERS DEFENSE

1. Pick one other PC. This character protected you from harm recently, and you feel indebted to him for saving your life.

2. Pick one other PC. She thinks you are an incredibly selfish person, perhaps based on her belief that you always save yourself first.

3. Pick one other PC. You once fought on opposite sides of a combat.

4. Pick one other PC. This character seems to be a jinx for you. Whenever she is next to you, the difficulty of defense tasks is increased by one step. However, you're the opposite for her—when you're next to her, the difficulty of her defense tasks is decreased by one step.

MASTERS WEAPONRY

1. Pick one other PC. That character shows potential in the use of your weapon. You would like to train her, but you're not necessarily qualified to teach (that's up to you), and she might not be interested (that's up to her).

2. Pick one other PC. If she is within immediate range when you're in a fight, sometimes she helps, and sometimes she accidentally hinders (50% chance either way, determined per fight). When she helps, you gain +1 to all attack rolls. When she hinders, you suffer a –1 penalty to attack rolls.

3. Pick one other PC. You once saved his life, and he clearly feels indebted to you. You wish he didn't; it's all just part of the job.

4. Pick one other PC. This person recently mocked your combat stance. How you deal with this (if at all) is up to you.

MURDERS

1. Pick one other PC. That character knows your real identity, profession, and background. To all others, the truth about you is a closely guarded secret.

2. Pick one other PC. You were approached by someone recently who wanted to hire you to take that character out. You haven't yet decided whether to take the job or warn her that her life's in danger.

3. Pick two other PCs. One night after perhaps too much celebrating, you loudly claimed responsibility for a murder you didn't commit. These two characters were the only ones who heard. Whether they believe you or not is up to them.

4. Pick one other PC. That character is the one who got you started down the path of taking lives, whether he knows it or not.

Hunts With Great Skill, page 65
Leads, page 66
Lives in the Wilderness, page 67
Masters Defense page 68
Masters Weaponry, page 69
Murders, page 70

In certain situations, if the story warrants it, you could allow the character to choose an additional focus. So a Graceful jack who Commands Mental Powers at "seventh tier" becomes a Graceful jack who Commands Mental Powers and Never Says Die. In this case, the character must take the first-tier ability at "seventh tier," the second-tier ability at "eighth tier", and so on, in order.

RAGES

1. Choose one other PC. You feel strangely protective toward that character and don't want to see her come to harm.

2. Pick one other PC. That character knows a secret about your past that is tied to your Frenzy ability.

3. Pick one other PC. The first time you went into a frenzy was in an attempt to save that character's loved one from an attack. You failed, partly because of your inexperience.

4. Choose one other PC. He is terrified by your rage and sometimes can't help but flee at inopportune times.

RIDES THE LIGHTNING

1. Pick one other PC. This character has been your friend for a long time, and you have learned to bring her along when you ride the lightning. If the character is standing right next to you, you can take her with you when you use the Bolt Rider or Electrical Flight powers. (Normally, neither ability allows you to transport other creatures.)

2. Pick two other PCs. You know about an important connection between them that even they don't know about.

3. Pick one other PC. This character has interesting ideas about electricity and how it can be harnessed. If you are trained in the numenera, you gain an asset on any numenera-based task after you talk to this character for an hour.

4. Pick one other PC. He has the worst luck with electrical devices of anyone you've ever met. You want to help him, but you aren't sure how or even whether he will be open to your assistance.

TALKS TO MACHINES

1. Pick one other PC. That character seems to have a terrible relationship with machines—or at least the machines that you communicate with. If she is next to a machine that you interact with in a friendly manner, that machine is treated in all ways as being one level lower than normal (unless doing so benefits you or her, in which case the level does not change).

2. Pick one other PC. He seems especially leery of you, though this could just be your perception.

3. Pick one other PC. She has a small machine among her equipment but won't tell you any details about it or let you see it.

4. Pick one other PC. You know that this character knows an incriminating or embarrassing secret about you, and you hope that he doesn't reveal it.

WEARS A SHEEN OF ICE

1. Pick one other PC. Due to a quirk of the numenera, if that character is standing next to you when you use your Ice Armor ability, he is also protected by a sheen of ice. (He does not get the added protection of your Resilient Ice Armor ability.)

2. Pick one other PC. For a reason unknown to you, her very presence seems to heat the air around you, making it more difficult to command the powers of ice and cold. If she is within immediate range, her presence occasionally makes it one step more difficult to hit a target with a focus ability.

3. Pick one other PC. That person is especially susceptible to the cold that radiates from you. How he handles that vulnerability is up to him.

4. Pick one other PC. The two of you have a long history and almost always disagree about the best way to handle situations.

WIELDS POWER WITH PRECISION

1. Pick one other PC. You've placed an immutable, one-time ward that renders her immune to the esoteries you perform unless she wants to be affected.

2. Pick one other PC. Due to some quirk of the numenera, you can occasionally (and accidentally) share your powers with him, thus

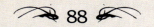

reducing the difficulty of any task he attempts using his esoteries by one step.

3. Pick one other PC. That character doesn't seem to trust or like you, but you feel compelled to win her over.

4. Pick one other PC. You've noticed that he has a book in his possession that you'd very much like to study, but you're unsure how to ask him about it.

WIELDS TWO WEAPONS AT ONCE

1. Pick one other PC. You have trained with this character so much that if the two of you stand back to back in a fight, you both gain a +1 bonus to Speed defense tasks.

2. Pick one other PC. This character always seems to inadvertently foil your actions, or at least make them more difficult. If she is within immediate range, the difficulty of any action related to this focus that you take is increased by one step.

3. Pick one other PC. You recently had a weapon go missing, and you're becoming convinced that he took it. Whether or not the character actually did so is up to him.

4. Pick one other PC. You used to dislike him immensely, but as you get to know him, you're growing fond of him against your better judgment.

WORKS MIRACLES

1. Pick one other PC. This character quietly suspects that you're a messiah or supernatural being. You can choose whether or not you're aware of his suspicion.

2. Pick one other PC. He knows a secret of yours, and you desperately hope that he doesn't tell anyone.

3. Pick one other PC. She believes that you cured someone close to her of a deadly disease, and she is grateful. You aren't sure whether you actually helped or if that person wasn't as sick as he claimed.

4. Pick one other PC. You secretly believe that she might be a hypochondriac, and you're never sure whether she actually needs your help.

WORKS THE BACK ALLEYS

1. Pick one other PC. The character knew you beforehand and convinced you to leave your life of crime for other pursuits—at least temporarily.

2. Pick one other PC. A while back, you attempted to "borrow" something from her, but she busted you in the process. You managed to convince her that it was a simple misunderstanding, but she may not entirely trust you.

3. Pick one other PC. You never seem to be able to hide so that he can't see you.

4. Pick one other PC. She knows your real identity (if it's a secret) or that you work undercover (if it's a secret) and has kept the knowledge to herself so far. It's up to her whether she continues to do so.

SWITCHING DESCRIPTORS AND FOCI AFTER CHARACTER CREATION

As the campaign goes along, it's possible that a player might want to switch the descriptor or focus that she chose when creating her character.

It's best if these changes occur organically rather than being forced. In other words, a character's descriptor changes because something happened in the game to change her, or her focus changes because a new opportunity arose in the course of play. (Don't do it if a player wants to change just for the sake of variety or to become more powerful in the current situation. In these cases, the GM should have the player make a new character instead.)

Changing a descriptor is both easy and appropriate, particularly with some of the new descriptors found in this book. For example, in the course of play, a Strong glaive's father is killed by a terrible villain. The glaive is fueled now by revenge. This story event could easily justify the glaive changing his descriptor to Vengeful or Driven. If he became a terrible person because of it, he might take the

Wields Two Weapons at Once, page 75
Works Miracles, page 75
Works the Back Alleys, page 76

As with everything, switching descriptors and foci should be worked out between the player and the GM. The best play experiences come from good communication.

It's likely that gameplay will become less satisfying after a while spent at tiers above sixth. Sixth-tier characters are already legendary in their prowess. Those who become even more powerful won't find most situations very challenging.

Dishonorable descriptor. Likewise, a Learned nano who falls into a vat of acid might become Hideous or Mad.

Of course, these characters lose their old descriptor and any benefits it conveyed, but that can be a part of the story, too. The Strong glaive who is now a Vengeful glaive stopped exercising and physically pushing his body. He might still be strong, but it's not his defining characteristic—he's not as strong as he was. He's vengeful instead. Likewise, the Learned nano forgets some of her schooling and loses her focus on such pursuits due to the accident that made her hideous.

There's no limitation on the number of times a character can change his descriptor. For example, if the aforementioned glaive achieves his vengeance, maybe he goes back to being strong—as long as it fits the story.

Switching a focus is a bit trickier, and the story reason is probably more awkward. How does a jack who Carries a Quiver become a jack who Bears a Halo of Fire? The change likely involves time to train and a story reason. Perhaps the jack trained at a monastery she found in the hills where they specialize in "fire magic," or maybe she discovered some fire-related numenera. Perhaps she was kidnapped by strange forces and bathed in weird energies. It's Numenera, so almost anything is possible. You just have to work at it a bit.

Focus changes should occur only when a character attains a new tier, and it probably shouldn't be allowed more than once per character.

Mechanically, the new focus does not "overwrite" the old focus the way a new descriptor replaces an old descriptor. Instead, the old focus abilities remain, and at the new tier, the character gains an ability from the new focus, but the ability must come from a tier lower than the one just attained. For example, if our jack who Carries a Quiver begins to Bear a Halo of Fire at third tier, she keeps her first-tier and second-tier abilities from carrying a quiver, and for her third-tier ability,

Customizing Foci, page 118

she chooses either the first-tier or the second-tier ability from Bears a Halo of Fire (probably the first-tier ability, because that makes more sense). When she reaches fourth tier, she chooses from the first three tier abilities of Bears a Halo of Fire (although obviously she can't choose the ability she already selected). The character always chooses new abilities from tiers lower than the one she attains in her new focus. This means that the only way to get the sixth-tier ability of a focus is to start with that focus.

A character can't choose abilities from her former focus. Once the change is made, it's made.

TIERS ABOVE SIXTH

It will take a good long campaign to get a character up to the sixth tier. But what if you want to keep playing the character after that point? There is no seventh tier. Neither character types nor foci go beyond sixth.

However, you can simulate continued advancement quite easily. Allow characters to continue to pay for character benefits (4 XP each) as normal, with the following caveats:

• Do not allow characters to increase their Effort beyond 6. Instead, let them choose another skill or an alternative ability, such as adding 2 to their recovery rolls, reducing the cost of wearing armor, or selecting a new fighting move, esotery, or trick of the trade.

• Do not allow a character to have an Edge higher than 6 in any one stat.

• When a character gains four benefits, he gains a new tier. At that point, allow him to choose another ability suited to his character type (esoteries for nanos, fighting moves for glaives, or tricks of the trade for jacks). Further, allow him to choose any ability (of any tier) from the customizing foci ability options in the Numenera corebook.

CHARACTER PORTRAITS

Character portraits on this and the following pages are designed to be printed out and used on your character sheet for inspiration and ideas. They fit as-is onto the official Numenera character sheet but may be resized to fit other character sheets as needed.

CHARACTER OPTIONS INDEX

KEY: C = Numenera corebook   O = Character Options

MORE FROM THE NINTH WORLD

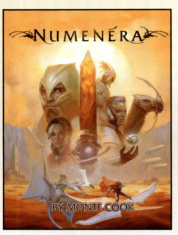

NUMENERA COREBOOK

The definitive guide for Numenera and the product that started it all, the corebook offers streamlined rules, intuitive character creation, an evocative setting, and GMing advice in a beautiful, full-color hardcover book.

416 pages. $59.99. MCG001

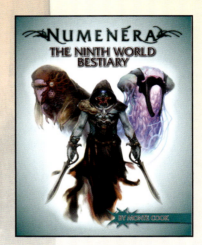

THE NINTH WORLD BESTIARY

This full-color hardcover creature book is lavishly illustrated, featuring creatures and some unique characters to use in Numenera games. A must-have for any Numenera GM.

160 pages. $39.99 MCG004

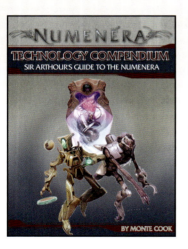

TECHNOLOGY COMPENDIUM: SIR ARTHOUR'S GUIDE TO THE NUMENERA

This full-color hardcover book is a manual of technology. Named in honor of Arthur C. Clarke and his "indistinguishable from magic" quote, it includes hundreds of new items and all kinds of wild, imaginative technologies.

160 pages. $39.99 MCG005

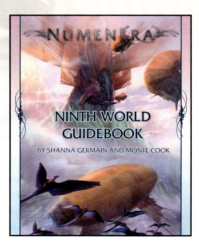

THE NINTH WORLD GUIDEBOOK

This full-color hardcover setting guide, building on what's in the Numenera corebook, brims with art and maps, presented in the style of a traveler's guide. Full of new adventures, creatures, and items, it also provides great ideas, stories, characters, and concepts for creating your next amazing campaign.

256 pages. $49.99 MCG006